A DANGEROUS PROFESSION

Also by Frederick Busch

Frederick Busch

A DANGEROUS PROFESSION

A Book About the Writing Life

ST. MARTIN'S PRESS ❦ NEW YORK

Production Editor: David Stanford Burr

Design by Ellen R. Sasahara

These essays, often in substantially altered form, originally appeared in the following publications: "My Father's War in *Five Points;* For the Love of a Princess of Mars" and "A Relative Lie" in *The Threepenny Review;* "The Writer's Wife" in *Los Angeles Times Book Review;* "The Floating Christmas Tree," "Melville's Mail," "The Language of Starvation," and "Even the Smallest Position" in *When People Publish: Essays on Writers and Writing;* "Bad" in *Ploughshares;* "The Rub" in *Georgia Review;* "Suitors by Boz" in *Gettysburg Review;* "Terrence Des Pres" in *TriQuarterly;* "The Unscrupulous Purity of Graham Greene" in *GQ;* "The Desert in the Bed" in *Denver Review* and *Why I Like This Story;* "Hemingway's Sentence" in *New York Times Book Review.*

Library of Congress Cataloging-in-Publication Data

Busch, Frederick.
    A dangerous profession : a book about the writing life
Frederick Busch.
        p. cm.
    ISBN 0-312-19255-X
    1. Busch, Frederick, 1941–   —Authorship.   2. Books and
reading.   3. Authorship.   4. Criticism   I. Title.
    PS3552.U814D3   1998
    808'.02—dc21   98-7329
                                                                CIP

First Edition: November 1998

10 9 8 7 6 5 4 3 2 1

CONTENTS

Contents / viii

Part One

Rightly or wrongly all remembrance of things past is fiction.

—Ernest Hemingway

MY FATHER'S WAR

THE MAPS IN the 1945 West Publishing Company pocket diary that my father carried in the war are gathered at the end of the little leather book. My father was very much a man of maps. During World War II, as a sergeant in the Tenth Mountain Division, an elite outfit trained and equipped for combat in snow and ice, on mountainous terrain, he was a scout. Carrying a radio and a carbine, he moved in advance of the infantry and artillery, calling howitzer and mortar fire down onto map coordinates that were often perilously close to his own position. He spoke infrequently of his war, but whenever he did, I asked him if he had been frightened. I found so much to be afraid of in quotidian adventures that I thought of his war as a time of always fighting fearfulness. Each time I asked, he said that he had been entirely certain that he could never be killed. According to him, he volunteered for service in the Tenth. According to him, he lied about his nearsightedness by memorizing the eye chart. According to my mother, he left for the war when he could have stayed with her and me. I had learned of others lying about their eyesight in films starring such men as William Bendix, Lloyd Nolan, and John Wayne; men memorized the eye charts because it was the right and morally true action, and because vision was not only about what a nearsighted man like my father could not see: he, and those heroes, the movies said, could *see*. I was reminded of my father's volunteering as I labored to keep from serving in Vietnam. I did not want to suffer at the hands of yahoos in the basic training that might kill me before any combat did. I did not want to leave my wife of so few months. I did not, finally, want to kill Asian people, any more than I thought they ought to be killing me; everything about that war was wrong, I thought (and think). And I am not imagining my father's disappointment at my despair over passing my first draftboard physical. I think he wanted me to want to go. I think he thought I might become a man, perhaps something closer to his idea of what men were, if I learned to enjoy, as he apparently had, overcoming the rigors of boot camp and fending off the rednecks who were puzzled or angered by Jews. He had invited them into the boxing ring, he told me, and they willingly went. He was in his thirties then, older than most of the men he called "boys," and, he told me, "After a round or two, when they tasted their own blood, they got more friendly."

When I was a sullen kid, he offered to teach me to box. In the cement-floored basement with its big, noisy oil burner—I had played in the coal bins near the old coal-burning furnace in the forties—he laced us in and offered instruction in the rudiments. He didn't draw blood. But he liked it (I could see that in his clenched teeth, the half smile: a simulated but possibly felt ferocity) as he pawed me with his jab and slapped me again and again with the open glove. I am not certain what the lesson was, but I knew as he nicely enough toyed with me, teaching me technique I would forget, that he was teaching me something else: *I am always holding back what you think you almost see. It is in me. It is always almost here.* Or maybe I am thinking of what I thought and felt when I was the father of teenaged sons.

He carried the pocket diary with him through his year of combat, 1945. Its publishers offered information one wouldn't need today. There is, in one table, a chart of mail time to foreign places from New York: thirteen days to Belgrade, Yugoslavia, and eighteen days to Leningrad, Russia. The price charts are as out-of-date as the maps—ten cents is the surcharge given for special-delivery mail weighing up to two pounds. A couple of pages in the back of the book have been torn away. I wonder when he did that, and what he sought to hide. It was his book, after all, and it was unlikely that anyone in his house or his office in Manhattan would search his wartime diary for clues—although that is precisely what I have done fifty years later. But he might have known more than most of us about hiding information, or about digging it out. And he might have had something to hide.

It seems entirely likely that he tore out the pages when he was preparing to die. I suspect that he did so in the 1970s, given his claim that he had been unfrightened of death. However, I find a note about V-J Day written in his hand. He knew that his outfit was to participate in the invasion of Japan, and he writes, "To be assured of the end of war—the end of the dread of death." He might have felt differently about fighting in Asia. Or maybe he was a secret from himself. He didn't dread death, and he also did, perhaps, and perhaps each secret side of himself did not know the other. He feared to die and knew he wouldn't be killed. But he almost was—he was blown up pretty badly—and it is possible that he was telling a lie he needed to tell and to hear. He lived, I think, in compartments—like the watertight compartments of submarines, like the cells of spy groups or the partisan cells of World War II. If one compartment is flooded by some of the billion tons of water outside, the rest might survive awhile. If you know only five members of your cell, you cannot tell captors or a witch-hunt committee or the FBI the names of anyone else in the underground; the damage, if you name the names, is limited to you and the other four. If you compartmentalize your nights and days—at 956 East Eighteenth Street in Brooklyn, or at the firm of Katz & Sommerich, Attorneys-at-Law, 120 Broadway in Manhattan—then *all* of your selves can't be caught.

He spent Christmas Eve of 1944, says his spiky, meticulous hand, on the train to Camp Patrick Henry in Norfolk, Virginia. On Wednesday, January third: "Called Home—Spoke to Mom, Freddy and Phyllis." I can see him, slender and balding, with sensuous lips and dreamy blue eyes, a handsome thirty-three-year old man who had been a beautiful boy, traveling in the dim train into a dark southern night in the time of both the festival about families and about the loss of time. Once stationed at Patrick Henry, he enters "Ditto," or sometimes "Do," under the date of each day he spent there. And then, on January fifth, with no reference to Europe (which is unmarked by him in the map section), he writes, "Train to Pier—Embarkation—U.S.S. General Meigs at P.M." The next day, he writes, "Shipboard—sailed at 12:30 P.M." There is something likable about the care with which he noted times and tended to his spellings and observed the forms—that "U.S.S." I wonder if the care about details was a stay against panic or whether he had concluded that a soldier kept a journal that was correct about dates and times and places and that left emotions out. I think of Hemingway, and my father's respect for his work, and how his Frederic Henry says, in *A Farewell to Arms:*

> I was always embarrassed by the words sacred, glorious, and sacrifice. . . . There were many words that

you could not stand to hear and finally only the names of places had dignity. Certain numbers were the same way and certain dates and these with the names of the places were all you could say and have them mean anything. Abstract words such as glory, honor, courage, or hallow were obscene beside the concrete names of villages, the numbers of roads, the names of rivers, the numbers of regiments and the dates.

The next nine days say "Ditto." The tenth says that, too, and then "Gibraltar a.m.—African Coast." I think he must have smiled his broad grin, the boy from Brooklyn, to see that shore crawl past the rail.

After much more "Ditto," they anchored off Naples. He notes, "Vesuvius—Pompeii." On Friday, January nineteenth: "Tried Red Cross for cable—n.g." No good: He couldn't cable home to say he'd survived the Atlantic crossing. In LCI 194, a Landing Craft Infantry, they "began journey North—Bad weather—turned back." Then, in entries confined to place names, and with a few verbs—*docked* and *spent*—he describes his movements in LCI 194 from Naples to Pozzuoli, north past Elba to Leghorn. Wednesday, January twenty-fourth: "Truck convoy to 3rd staging area—Rain at night." Then "Ditto," then "Ditto," then "Ditto."

On Sunday, January twenty-eighth, he writes, "On to the Front," then "Lizzano in Belvedere—Billet in Theatre—on floor." In darker ink, perhaps with firmer pressure, he writes, "One year since induction in U.S. Army." And, with two notes about "Mail call," he spends four days of "Ditto," which, on Friday, February second, he changes to "Same," as if to combat the sameness of his experience.

Think of yourself at the front in a war, waiting for combat, for his was a combat outfit. Think of knowing that you will soon, at any dawn or dusk, go into battle. What would you record, should you choose to record anything at all? Here, among the thousands in the Tenth awaiting their first fight and possibly their death, is Benjamin J. Busch. He was given no middle initial by his parents but was renamed Busch, Benjamin J., by the army to distinguish him, alive and dead, from another Busch, Benjamin, on the rolls. There is his life with Phyllis and me and his parents, his sisters Ann and Rose, his brother, Jack, his legal career, and whatever else concerned him in civilian life. There is the matter of climbing rocks while carrying the heavy radio over booby traps into mortar fire. He is in a kind of suspension. It is "Same" to him, and we cannot know, by looking at his pages, whether he bathed, and how or what he ate. I wonder what he dreamed about. He will not tell. He notes his "1st week at front" with no reference to explosions on the skyline or the condition of his bowels and brains. There is no statement about death or fear; they are all I can imagine myself imagining. Everything is "Same," except when he receives a cable from one of his sisters, then from my mother, though he doesn't report what they say to him, or how he feels.

On Wednesday, February 14, 1945, in his second week at the front, after ten days of "Same": "St. Valentine's Day Corsage & cable should be delivered to Phyllis today." Three days later, he goes on "Patrol up front at Farne." All most of us know about patrols are breathless moments in movies or books. He doesn't confirm or deny what we know.

Sunday, February eighteenth, begins "Same," notes his "3rd Week at Lizzano"; on the nineteenth: "Attack on Ridge near Farne" and "Ridge is taken"; he was one of the takers, but the passive voice separates him from the dangers within which he writes. On the twentieth "Attack continues" and "Air Support" and "Belvedere is Taken." On the twenty-first: "Battle continues" and "We advance up Mt—Shelling around road." He told of that road. He spoke of their having to cross it one at a time because the large German mortars were so accurate and were backed up by heavy machine-gun fire. He spoke of men closing their eyes and running. And when I asked him—what a frightened child I must have been—if he had been scared, he turned the corners of his mouth down happily and told me, "Nah." On the twenty-second: They "Advance past Gaggis" and receive "Shelling of our positions." He "Rec'd letters from home." Next day: "Same Positions—Battle continues.—" On the twenty-fourth: "Same" and, in a shakier, hastier hand, "Rec'd letters from home & pictures of Freddy."

The next week, his handwriting changes from day to day, as does the pressure of the pen. "Attack & Counter attack continues," he writes on February twenty-fifth, and he is proud that news of his division is "flashed to America." He receives mail and pictures, then notes, "We change positions," which seems to be in response to shelling, so, on the twenty-sixth, they change positions again and he notes a "shower bath & change of clothes." The Tenth, he records, is commended by General Hayes, the shelling continues, and, on the twenty-eighth, "Shelling during night with some landing uncomfortably close." That "uncomfortably" is the first acknowledgment of real danger. "Same" follows "Same," and then, on March third: "Push begins at 0700—heavy artillery fire through day and night We prepare to move forward—Infantry gains its objective," the artillery scout notes. On Sunday, March fourth, they advance and "Al Strilecky & I spend night on top of Mt. Terminale—dead & equipment around." He is there the next night and then he notes, "Left flank—400 yds from enemy." The next day they are "raked by mortar fire both crests & drawer from top to halfway down." Howitzer shells land around them: "Heaviest shelling yet during the night—landing very close." In the late afternoon, their "arty [for artillery] fired leaflets & addressed Hun lines by P.A. system": They were that close.

On March eighth, still at Iola, mortar shells land near their dugouts, "ruining equipment 20 ft. from mine." They move out of the range of the mortars on their flank, they are joined by some infantry, and their positions are "straightened & consolidated," which means that their lines of fire are reorganized: They are within small-arms range of the Germans.

After receiving artillery fire early in the next week, they relocate to what he calls a "rest camp." He does not mention the radio, the calling in of the fire on the Germans, the scampering through or sheltering from the incessant deadly mortars and heavier artillery. They make it to Montecantini, the location of the rest camp of the Fifth Army. He rents a private room in a hotel for two dollars. On Friday, March sixteenth, he celebrates: "shower & new clothes—Barbershop & works.—Tour of town—vino & plenty." The next night, another bar crawl, a "tour of town," and movies, and on Sunday, March eighteenth, after staying "up to 1:30," celebrating, he is sent "Back to front."

Their week begins at Brasa with scattered shelling, and then he hikes—his verb—to an observation post "within German observation." The next night, their patrol activity is visible by the light of the phosphorous tracer shells of the German machine-gun fire. They take artillery shelling. The next night, he is carried by jeep to patrol another area; he sees four men in an enemy patrol. There are "Frequent flares" and "Heavy enemy mortar shelling." They are moved to Pietra Colera, then Florence and a rest camp for several days, then back to Pietra Colera. They reconnoiter, they take mortar and artillery fire— sixty German rockets land near their observation post at Gualandi—and he notes, "Some close shelling—farm barn roof 20 yds from billet" and "Terrific barrage for one hour—": the closest he comes to what he won't directly express, the sense of death, the smell of fear, the hugeness of the force of the explosions, and the nakedness of flesh.

The following week is one of patrols, receiving barrages,

and more patrols. There is a change of positions, a preparation for an attack. On Friday, April thirteenth, "H hour," he reports, "is delayed." On the fourteenth, with the Second of the Eighty-sixth, at 0830, after preparatory "Planes & arty barrage—Advance with Col. Townsend—Up to Rocco di Roffino."

At home, after the war, he dreamed of himself tied to a tree. Snakes crawled toward him. They wore German helmets. He sought therapy in painting, and he had something of a hand. The two paintings he framed are of mountains. One is seen from below and is wintry, pretty, a convincing-enough, if conventional, peak. I wonder if it is the mountain his division scaled, at night, to engage the German ski troops. The other mountain he painted is seen from above, as a hawk might see; a bit of the hawk's wing frames the view, and the point of view suggests detachment. He read Freud, he told me when I was in college, because he wanted to work his way out of the nightmares. When he spoke of the war, my mother interrupted, always, to tell him that it was harmful for him to discuss what he so clearly needed to discuss. The Freud worked, he managed to convey to me; the dreams, he claimed, went away. There is evidence that the dreams continued, and that he spoke of them, and to someone other than my mother, someone who labored to relieve him of their burden. But he told us that they went away.

That rhythm of suppression and release, the tension between obedience to forms of gravity and the finding of a way to soar, the need to say the story and the requirements of silence— those are the man.

On April fifteenth, he was blown up by a booby trap on a mountain trail. The lieutenant he was with walked ahead of him and stepped on the spring release and was torn to pieces. My father was wounded in the foot, groin, and hand. This is the witness borne by the father to his son, an unusually intimate conversation of the early 1960s, an occasion rarely repeated.

The privately public self, in the diary of 1945, has this to report, in a shaky hand that is the pictorial equivalent of gasping. For Sunday, April fifteenth: "After Midnight down to guide up Replacements—Wounded by Mine—15th Evac. Hosp." There is no reference to trauma or pain, to his wounds, to the men who carried him to safety, or to the officer ahead of him who was so terribly dissolved. The next day's entry: "15th Evac Hosp." I am astonished not only by the taciturnity of these entries but also by his ability to force himself to make them. He reports to himself, one bit of him intoning his noninformation to the other. Tuesday, April seventeenth: "70th Genl Hosp near Poistoia," and I cannot tell whether he was stabilized or worse or needed further surgery. There, he is "Given Purple Heart." The next day, he reports his mailing address, as if telling his wife how to find him, and as if it is also he himself who needs to know. He repeats, the total entry for each of the next eleven days, "70th G.H." Within a total of fifteen days, he is discharged and is back with the artillery battery for which he was a scout. On Wednesday, May second: "Armistice announced." By the fifth, he walks to Riva Ridge, gets a big batch of mail that followed him, and was "Given Good Conduct Medal."

They move to Lake Garda, they are on alert, there is mail censorship—which he notes but doesn't complain about—and then they move to a point about five miles from Yugoslavia, where they await the Allied decision on supporting Tito. There is nothing about communism, only that the people are "more Slavic." They camp there for eight days. He goes to Venice, on May twenty-ninth, on a one-day pass. Then he is back with his outfit for a week, and then, for June sixth, this: "To Hospital near Cividole for Therapy—left hand." It is, of course, not preceded by reports from himself to himself about his disabilities or pain. Two days later: "6th Gen. Hosp. near Bologna arrive atr 4:30 P.M." and then "Same." The next day: "Therapeutic treatment," and the next says, "Operated on for removal of fragment from scrotum." The entry for June twelfth says, "Same. My 33rd birthday." Twelve days of "Same" later, he "received P.B.'s old wedding ring," which he asked her to send because his had been cut off his hand. He doesn't comment on his need for it, or, in fact, on its removal. He doesn't refer to how his nurses worked his fingers—it was like having the bones broken every day, he told me—against the hardening of calcium deposits after his surgery. That is who he is—these separate, hidden men.

Aboard the *Blue Ridge Victory*, no "U.S.S." this time, he tastes "first fresh milk," and celebrates lettuce, celery, and olives. He notes my fourth birthday on August first, cites but doesn't complain about the rough seas, and reports on sightings of "flying fish, porpoises, sharks, sea turtles, plovers or petrels"—the kid from Brooklyn among the exotic fauna. He writes, "Land Ho!" on August ninth," is fed "steak and all," and says, "I call Phyll!!" He is given his furlough papers and on August eleventh is at "Penn Station by 11 P.M. Speed! It's wonderful." His version of it is that he is "Home by midnight and I meet Phyll walking toward me on 18th near I." His version of it has her necessarily at home with their child, but each is urged toward the other, and after midnight, by the streetlights, he sights her as she seeks him. Her version has them walking on different sides of the street and his walking past, not recognizing her.

After the war, back with his firm, he traveled by subway to work and then he walked, from the Chambers Street station in lower Manhattan to the building at 120 Broadway in which his firm had its offices. He had been with Katz & Sommerich since he was a law clerk, and he rose to be a senior partner, and, at last, he was the only living remnant of the firm. Katz and Sommerich were Jewish international lawyers in a field that had been notoriously Anglo-Saxon. He never told us that he had changed his name because of his profession, but he and his brother did indeed change the name—Buschlowitz—that Sam and Dorothy brought from Minsk, in Russia, to its present German-seeming form. You can follow him on a subway map or a map of New York from Flatbush, over the East River on the Manhattan Bridge, to Chambers Street, and the neighborhood distinguished by the beauty of Trinity Church and the Treasury, made charming by its narrow streets, made gray by the office buildings that seal away the light of the sky. But then he would vanish, and you would need to know that he had cut away from the marked route and had gone to a restaurant in his building, the Savarin, to be served, apparently, by the same woman who had served him for years, where he ate a second breakfast and read one of the many newspapers he read each day.

Maybe, that is, he ate breakfast and read the papers. My mother joked, not laughing, that he lived a secret life at the office. In his early days, she had dined with him and clients and had jeopardized a relationship by speaking bitterly to a client's wife or girlfriend. Miss MacMullan, an executive secretary of broad experience and great intelligence, on whom he relied with deep trust, and who was always referred to as Mac, had advised him to keep his wife away from clients thereafter, and he had faithfully followed Mac's advice. There was secrecy in where he went and what he did in the mornings, and I have to wonder about his trips to serve Mr. Tsung and Mr. Tsang, clients in the 1960s and 1970s, who were married to relatives of Sun Yat-sen and who had brought fortunes with them from Taiwan; often he went off to Westchester, ostensibly to serve them. He traveled for other clients, the House of 4711, in Cologne, and let's call him Z, an eccentric and wealthy European, and for interests in pre-Castro Cuba. He told us where he had been, and we assumed that the names and the places on the map were true.

No matter where he traveled, no matter where he lived, he also lived in a place that was not on any map. He descended in the morning from his private bathroom on the third floor of our house in Brooklyn, and he ate his peanut butter on toast while sipping coffee. He wore a Brooks Brothers suit of dark gray or brown or blue with a good necktie and a good shirt. He was stylish and dapper within the limits trial lawyers usually set. He left to walk to the subway after kissing us good-bye. He smelled very good and his cheeks were smooth. When he reappeared, at about seven at night, his cheek was bristly, his shirt rumpled, his tie quickly loosened or pulled off. We could call him on his busiest days and be spoken to cordially, patiently, with affection. Mac and his secretary, Miss Bertha Schwab, spoke to us as if we were the boss's kid. It took me years to understand we were. Sometimes he came home with stories of courtroom adventures, of a loss of temper in the office or even before a judge. It was clear that he loved litigation as much as he enjoyed being telephoned by clients on matters unrelated to the case that had brought them to his office; clients would ask for advice on the purchase of a piece of land, or even a car, and though his practice was about foreign law—his book is called *The Pleading and Proof of Foreign Law*—he was asked to advise his clients on their interior lives, the state of their investments, the progress of their divorce. His voice was rumbly and his mind quick; he was the soul of gallant manners—a Victorian man—whom women were drawn to even in his old age.

He woke before the rest of the house and went from his bed in my parents' large bedroom—they did not sleep in the same bed from the time of my first remembering—and went up the narrow stairs outside their bedroom door to the attic—a third floor divided into two large bedrooms and a bathroom. They kept one room as a spare bedroom, while the other, the size of their own, stored knapsacks and camping equipment and, if I remember correctly, the two army-surplus barracks beds once used by my brother and me. My grandparents lived there for a while in the 1950s, and after my grandmother died and my grandfather went to live with his other son, Jack, my father took to using the attic bathroom as his own. It was to that room, painted a resolutely cheerful yellow, that my father went every day. He had privacy there, and the smells of the 4711 cologne that was beginning to earn him a good deal of money. He stopped having a body in the house with the rest of us, choosing to bathe in the tub upstairs rather than shower where the rest of us did.

So, early, he went up. As we were waking, he came down to dress. As we were breakfasting, he left. As we were sitting down to dinner, he returned. He appeared, he disappeared, and then he reappeared. He was easy and affectionate with us, concerned for the life we each had led in his absence, but removed nevertheless, mysterious because of his own, distant-feeling life.

His father was small, strong, and sweet-dispositioned. A master carpenter in Russia, he had come once to the States and then returned to Belorussia because he hadn't liked it here. I don't know why he came back with Dorothy to live at first in Detroit, then raise his family in Brooklyn. Before he had come to the States, he had been his Anarchist cell's pistol keeper. He never married Dorothy, refusing bourgeois convention. When he was with us, he was no Turgenev character, but the gentle, silent man who smiled as we spoke, who let us doodle or do homework with his stubs of carpenter's pencil. He was sectioned off, like his son and like his wife, who despised my mother (and was despised in return) but whose sturdy body and square, solid peasant's face—always smiling for me—were ever at my disposal. She took me to the Midwood Theater on Avenue J to see *The Thing*, a frightening film of the fifties. Earlier, she had sat with me in our living room, interposing her un-comprehending smile—for she spoke little English—between me and Orson Welles's fearful laughter on the radio when "The Shadow" came on and he asked who knew what evil lurked in the hearts of men.

My father knew. For after a prelude to war that may have been full of feeling and incident, but which he reported as "Ditto" or "Same," and after a wounding that left him dream-ing of serpents in German helmets, and which he reported in his diary as essentially a series of locations, he came home dreaming of honey, but he found he was smelling corruption and swallowing bile. His hopes were clear, and emotion finally tugged at his pen: He writes, on August twelfth, "From here on to Sept. 13—it will be home and home with Phyll & Fred." Then he says this:

> With all the rest and inactivity we have had since Peace in Europe this is still the first relaxation of mind and body for these comparatively few months that seemed interminable years. How easy it is to spring back to old surroundings when they are peaceful and imbued with all the love and affection that surrounds me in my home. I am like the cat purring before a warm fire, reluctant to move away from the hearth.

He continues—it seems to all be an entry for the twelfth that covers page after little page:

> Actually I dread meeting the people and friends and acquaintances that I know. And later events support my feeling. They are of a different world that neither knows nor tries to imagine what has happened. I am

hurt to find how they think and act. It seems so useless to talk to them and difficult to find a common
ground. I find it easier to dislike people. I find it
more difficult to conceive of people with kindness
and goodness in their hearts. . . . [He refers here to
a dinner with friends thought to be intellectuals.]
The so-called advanced can be so cruel and without
understanding. And everything they have done and
others shows as a selfish concentration in the war
years on objects away from the immediate welfare of
war veterans. The old cry of the fate of the soldiers
being the same as the fate of the workers is of course
true but too palpably uneven—an immediate bal-
ancing of the scales to provide for the competitive
life is a necessity—to provide for the student, the
family man, the person without a reserve but immediate expenses.

And here is a troubled dispatch, then, in this seamless entry,
from one side of the man to another—from the purring bourgeois to the detester of the bourgeoisie, complete with a little
Marxist baggage—"The old cry . . . is of course true but"—that
he wishes to dump as much as he seems to need to carry it. He
is so distraught that his punctuation falters, his syntax slips. But
then he stops himself and says:

But everything I have wanted and thought of—I
have had on my furlough—the company of Phyll &
Fred—the unhurried feel of home—a few movies &
dinners out—the simple things that meant so
much—the foods & drinks and pleasures that were
the oasis of the dryness of time. Once again to be
able to speak & think aloud to a person who thinks
and feels as I do. And of course how swell it was to

have the gift of V.J. day during my furlough. To be
assured of the end of war—the end of the dread of
death.

He writes of his reassurance that he can avoid "the emptiness of
a useless trip to Japan," and says that his division will remain in
America "for the balance of my Army career which I want to be
as short as possibly can be. Paints become the order of the day
will continue to be until that eventful discharge."

His self-administered therapy isn't discussed, although it's
referred to again in September, when he is transferred to another unit and must spend time in Colorado awaiting his discharge from the service. Now, in Brooklyn, with paints the
order of the day, he is purring of home and peace and dream-
ing of snakes in German helmets. We would now say that he
was suffering from posttraumatic combat stress disorder, I suppose. His bleak sense of human generosity seems to have been
formed by that experience—or, perhaps, that experience helped
to define what was in him from the start. He was optimistic in
ways—believing the best of me and my brother when others
didn't, reaching for his pretty, voluptuous wife, working his little garden like a Brooklyn burgher—and in ways, he was closed
off and brooding. He wanted more than Brooklyn, the brother,
the Yiddish of his parents, the sad beauty of his sisters; he
wanted what was elegant, cosmopolitan, rich. He walked
the woods on field trips with my mother, but he also walked the
lobby of the Georges V in Paris, and he knew, over the years,
which he preferred.

It was usually my mother who asked my father to chart their
course, since her sense of direction was unreliable. But when
they were first married, in the 1930s, my mother told me, it was
he who asked her. He had moved into her apartment on
Eleventh Street. In the tone of her telling, he had failed by not
providing an apartment of his own. On their first morning to-

gether as husband and wife, she rose and dressed and walked to the door.

"Where are you going?" he asked her.

"Oh," she said. "I forgot you were here," she proudly said she said.

This is the woman he must leave, he writes in his journal, when he must return, after his furlough at the end of the war, to his outfit in Colorado. It is September nineteenth: "Easy to feel terribly lonesome. I look at my pictures of Phyll & Freddy & fix them & arrange them." On the twenty-first, he is "Lonelier than hell. Must call home. Try but delay in calls is too great." He is interestingly discursive (for him) about his pain. On the next day: "Try to call home again. No answer—try again. Catch Phyll in late afternoon. A swell talk and I feel lots better." On the next day: "After all it won't be very long," and on the next day, with the news that accrued leave will hasten his departure for home: "Whoopee!" He catches a slow train; at home, he and Phyllis buy theater tickets and shop. They celebrate Phyllis's birthday by seeing Katherine Dunham dance— "not so hot." Sunday, October seventh: "Home." For the next thirteen days, "Ditto" is reduced to "do," and it is the sole entry for each day—not the warmth and joy of home, not the conviviality of someone who thinks as he does, and not the personal warmth, if there is any, that proves his wound to the loins is healed: My brother will be born nine months from now. He returns to Colorado, and then he comes home, some weeks later, and he writes, on Thursday, December 6, 1945, "Home Again! But for Good!"

Back to combat, then, in his mind: the dreams of serpents, the German helmets, the being tied to a tree. Walter Bernstein, reporting for *The New Yorker* of September 1944 on the mountain fighting in Italy, described his experience of being shelled—as my father was shelled five months later, before being wounded by a mine and undergoing two operations at once and two a little while later:

> But there is something about heavy artillery that is inhuman and terribly frightening. You never know whether you are running away from it or into it. It is like the finger of God. I felt cowardly and small at the base of this tremendous hill, walking alone on the floor of this enormous valley. I felt like a fly about to be swatted.

Ernie Pyle, a year before my father was in combat, described shelling in the mountains of Italy like this:

> The nagging of artillery eventually gets plain ag-gravating. It's always worse on a cloudy night, for the sounds crash and reverberate against the low ceiling. One gun blast alone can set off a continuous re-bounding of sound against clouds and rocky slopes that will keep going for ten seconds and more.
>
> And on cloudy nights you can hear shells tearing above your head more loudly than on a clear night. In fact, that night the rustle was so magnified that when we stopped to rest and tried to talk you couldn't hear what the other fellow said if a shell was passing overhead. And they were passing almost con-stantly.

To my father, it was "Heavy enemy mortar shelling" and "Terrific barrage for one hour." And then it was "Wounded by mine—15th Evac. Hosp.," and then the next day "15th Evac Hosp.," followed by twelve days described, in their entirety, as "70th Genl Hosp" and then "70th G.H." This was when they operated twice, when he worried about his potency, when he lay in pain, when they broke his hand.

His feelings here must be strong: Witness the serpents, the helmets, the tree. They are sealed away. His prose summons power to the description of his feelings when he is convinced he is no longer lonely; he celebrates his family and home. But among others, even in his home, he is angry and bitter, and his language darkly soars. And after his homecoming—"But for Good!"—after the compartmented diary days, after they have made love once, anyway, after thirty unfilled divisions of days in his diary, he writes this on the bottom of the last page in 1945, under a printed heading of "Memoranda":

> "But is a cheap kind of loving that
> can't admit the faults"
> > "Anything Can Happen"
> > George Papashvilly
> > & Helen Papashvilly

This small comfort—for what wound?—is buried, sealed away, in a compartment that is distant from his descriptions of his feelings, and which is even more distant from his notations of names, dates, and places. He was several people. He was secret from himself.

His final entry, except for names and addresses, suggests that either his wife brought to his attention in a painful way what she described as a fault—she did this with frequency—or he discovered a flaw, or worse, in her, and reminded himself with this quotation of his own requirement for loyalty to her. He struck me as keen on pain. He refused anesthetic when he underwent dental work. He was sunny with kids, he adored dogs, and he loved the gutsiness of brave athletes, yet he was the darkest, most brooding man I knew. When he didn't know we watched him, sometimes, his face fell into a mask of deep sorrow. He was fond of the bitterest passages in Schopenauer, and he remained convinced that humankind was essentially cruel.

In his diary, he misspelled the Papashvily in whose words he sought comfort. Helen was a Californian who ran bookshops and who, with George, owned one in Allentown, Pennsylvania. She married George, who was born in Soviet Georgia and who, after service in Persia during World War 1, lived in Constantinople until he emigrated to the United States. *Anything Can Happen*, written by Helen in George's dialect and published in 1945, tells George's stories of entering, surviving in, and then thriving in America. They are fragments of adventure or insight, characterized by a charming voice, a brave spirit, and an enterprising imagination. A typical paragraph reads like this:

> And now for me began one of the best times in my life, day by day I rode along and watched this wide beautiful country open before me. Day by day I found another new coin to add to my bag of gold that was America.

The stories are instructive, often sentimental. Goodness tends to triumph. Language, often referred to, and apparently a real factor in the life of everyone in the book, is at last seen as beside the point. Decency wins out, or is emphasized, despite the meanings of words. Good souls commune with good souls even though no one understands the other's language well. George lives for a while in Detroit, where Sam Buschlowitz also lived before he raised his family in Brooklyn. At the end, George owns a farm and flourishes. And while my father read this book, Sam and Dorothy were living on a farm in Monticello, New York.

So my father reads a book that suggests some of his father's experiences and that, because it narrates events of the Depression, cites fleeting disappointments in America. "It's a heart-tearing sight," George says, "to watch a person sicken and grow thin but oh so worse see a city die before your eyes. Yet that's what happened to Detroit the winter of 1932. First the factories went and then one by one the little shops . . . empty windows staring like dead eyes into deserted streets." Reflecting upon America's flaws compared with what America offers its citizens, George reflects, "But it's a cheap kind of loving that can't admit the faults." Perhaps, then, my father's use of the observation is to help him consider the nation that fails him, and other veterans. But it is the only quotation in the book. It ends the diary, and then there are addresses and telephone numbers, and then there are the stubs of the two sheets that were removed.

On one of them I can see fragments of the loops and lines of his handwriting. I think there is a story hidden there. Naturally, I think it is *the* story, the key to the secret. He's the secret to whom I returned again and again in my fiction, writing at least three versions—the latest, "Timberline," was published in *Georgia Review* in 1995—of the time he and I climbed Mount Washington in New Hampshire when I was a boy. A much earlier reference to the climb is in my story of 1976, in *Domestic Particulars*, "Trail of Possible Bones." A man named Abe in *Manual Labor* (1974) echoes my father, and so does a lawyer, described by his lover's daughter, in "Traveling Alone in Dangerous Places," a story in *Hardwater Country* (1979). He is the figure of darkness and light in "My Father, Cont.," a story from the same collection, and he is at the core of a story called "The Settlement of Mars" in *Too Late American Boyhood Blues* (1984). I think that he is an aspect of every charming, elusive, sturdy, and vanishing man I have written since my first novel was published in 1971.

You would think I'd have gotten him right by now, achieved some kind of satisfying resolution. But of course a writer cannot be satisfied: There *is* no satisfaction, because writing does not offer that emotion. The talent that drives a writer, the ambition to publish, the energy to continue—these are why he or she must write. The gift, if it is that, is also the goad. It is an appetite that feeds itself. One writes because of the writing, attempting to create, as John Gardner so perfectly said, "a vivid and continuous dream." One must be thoughtful as the writing procceds, for the sense of dream should grip the reader more than the writer. Yet the dreaminess seems to be tidal, it washes back upon the writer, and some of the sense of dream seems to enter whoever is creating it. And into that partial unconsciousness come the usual figures, again and again, like words upon which writers rely without realizing they have a basic, favored vocabulary. This is not a bad description of ghosts.

If a writer is honest, if what is at stake for him can seem to matter to his readers, then his work may be read. But a writer will work anyway, as I do, and as I have, in part to explore this terra incognita, this dangerous ground I seem to need to risk. I must want to travel there, but I'm uncertain why. I do it every day. I walk across the wet, cold grass, or the grass when it's withered by summertime heat, or the several feet of snow that lie upon it, and I walk up the barn ramp to the second-floor room, where I sit, a little breathless, and not from the walk, and I begin to work. Though I do not think of him (I think) every day as I start, his presence is powerful. Because in 1958, I had brought home from Muhlenberg a clumsy short story I thought of as good. In our living room in Brooklyn, he read it, then set it aside, saying, "Very nice." He meant to be kind, I'm certain. But he meant, more than that, to go on—and this is what he did—to tell me about his being wounded: how the officer ahead of him had been torn apart, and how he himself had thought at first that he was dead. He spoke of how men carried him down a mountain, setting his stretcher on the ground and covering his body with theirs when the German mortars opened up. During that descent, he reached down to his groin and brought his hand before his eyes. It was covered with blood and he thought at once, he said, of Jake Barnes and his wound. My father realized that he would be required to act with what he described for me as Barnes's "grace" now that he, too, was maimed.

I had never read *The Sun Also Rises*. My father didn't again read Hemingway except, I think, *The Old Man and the Sea* and those sad reports on his sentimental journey to Spain that became *The Dangerous Summer*. He didn't want to read Hemingway or anything else that was what he called "unhappy" or "make-believe"; he saw life as more dangerous than art, and he was sorrowful enough, I suppose. He read history—about the Civil War, the life of Lincoln, the Dead Sea Scrolls—and he read as many newspapers each day as he could. But he carried Hemingway's novel with him, as if it were part of his own life: At the time of his terrible trauma, he thought—according to him—of neither his God nor the Communist party, nor of his wife and his home. He thought of Jakes Barnes as if he were real.

That, of course, was why he rejected "make-believe" and unhappiness in novels. He believed in them. My father had received too much reality: It had tried to explode him. The reality of "make-believe" exploded him in another way, as well. He was very much like Nick Adams, after his experiences (and Hemingway's) in World War I, in "Big Two-Hearted River." Listen to Hemingway describe Nick's prayer: "He felt he had left everything behind, the need for thinking, the need to write, other needs. It was all back of him." The story proves "it" wasn't; "it" was with Nick nearly all of the time. And "it" was with my father.

And he wasn't finished. Folding his large hands, he asked me, my little story now ignored by both of us, whether I was truly serious, as serious as I claimed to be, about becoming a writer. I replied that I was. (How did I know?) And my father told me that I would need to know two facts.

"First," he said, "it's a terribly long, hard haul. People will try to ignore you and they'll try to hurt you if you keep them from ignoring you. What a writer needs most is energy. It's the most important thing you can have if you're really going to be a writer and outlast the bastards who'll try and stop you."

He almost never swore, and the "bastards" stunned me more than the advice itself—the importance of which I cannot over-rate.

"And second is," he went on, "you have to write dialogue. Nobody will believe your stories unless they have dialogue in them. People *talk,*" said my father, who so often didn't. "You should read Hemingway. Did you ever read Hemingway? *The Sun Also Rises* is a beautifully written book. Did you ever read it? There's a lot of dialogue in it that you could look at. You end up believing it—it's very moving."

For a man who sometimes didn't want to talk, or who felt discomfort in talking intimately, it was a pretty long speech. From a practical man, the man who had given up his painting but, like other practical people, was moved to tears by Ezio Pinza's "Some Enchanted Evening," the man who no longer read things "make-believe," such advice was an astonishment. Now it isn't. I know now how very vulnerable and always wounded he was. But then, in 1958, what he said was somehow extraneous to what I'd known of him. Still, and in spite of my ferocious lack of insight, my father's words sounded undeni-ably true. Every year afterward, they sounded truer. I thought for a while that he was the audience I would need to convince with my fiction, the only reader I needed to sway.

Whether I was reaching for him alone, for no one else, someone more objective than I will have to judge. I do know this: that on an autumn morning in 1997, I sat in the reference area of Colgate's library to check some spellings from the war diary. I was thinking, I thought, only professionally—that these considerations of Benjamin J. Busch would come first in a book of essays on writing and writers, that a copyeditor might well query some spellings and locations, that places in Italy had been renamed by the Fascisti, renamed by the occupying Allies, then possibly named again, and that I'd better get some facts straight. I sat with an atlas from the 1950s and with a sheaf of maps located for me by Colgate's head of reference, David Hughes. He'd been pleased to tell me about them, once I'd described this essay, and it was easy to see why: Some of the maps were based on RAF overflights, some on other sources, but all had been issued to American forces in 1944 by the United States Army. It seemed possible to us that I was holding copies of maps that my father had consulted.

I did not pretend to be the man in combat. I did not pretend to feel what he felt when he looked at his maps. I simply wanted to get the spellings right, and so I checked them in the index of the atlas—then, later, in several atlases—so that I could find the place on a smaller map in the front of the atlas and use that orientation to help me find the place on the larger 1944 maps; they were so large, and so confusing, such a blur of bright, poorly registered colors and spidery topographical whorls, that attempts to navigate with searching forefinger and blinking eye seemed nearly impossible.

I started where he did. From Naples, I traveled, or tried to, up to Puozzoli. He had misspelled it, but there we were: Pozzuoli. From there, past Elba, we had to find Leghorn, and there it was on the coast: Livorno. But, then, where was Lizzano? And which Belvedere had he meant? For there was Belvedere Marittimo, and then, two map pages later in the atlas, there was Belvedere di Spinallo. Conclusion: Make no conclusion; move on. But I was getting nervous. I have an awful sense of direction and my family knows that when I instruct us all to turn right, the proper course is unfailingly left. I have been known to become lost a hundred yards from a rented house in an unfamiliar neighborhood. Copyeditors have complained for years that in my work I conflate and compress and otherwise distort geography. And here I was, growing dry-mouthed because feeling, well, *lost*, a half an hour into a morning of research that I had looked forward to as tranquil, useful, and easier than writing prose.

I found no Gaggis. I found a Gaggiano and, two map pages later, across the country, a Gagliano de Capo. I shuttled from northern Italy, stalling near Brescia, which often seemed like the place he had fought in, then came to a dazed, flannel-tongued stumble fifteen or twenty miles outside of Rome.

He had referred to Iola. I realized, at last, that when he'd come to Livorno, he had sailed past Corsica, which is labeled Iola on the map, for "island." Near Monte Termonillo, which he called "Mt. Terminale," I did find Asola, and what was becoming a slow, silent panic abated. For not only had I begun to feel lost, as if alone and on foot in the vastness of the mapped nation but I also had begun, on drifting between northern and southern Italy, to doubt that he had been there. Was it possible, I remember asking myself, that he had made it up? The fear, the wound, the pain, all screened away from the self I had thought of as writing the diary—had it all been a fiction? But whom would he have sought to dupe? I wondered. Why? Monte Termonillo calmed me down. But I remember that equivalent of a child's hysterical crisis. In the library, during those moments, I spoke to two friends on the staff, and I smiled at a third. I was wailing, though, for a few hundred seconds, inside my skull.

Florence was fine, but what he called Pietra Colera didn't seem to exist. There was a Pierantonio, and I thought to make do with it. But Rocco de Roffino was also nonexistent, and so was Gualandi—I was able to find a Gualdo Tadino—but Riva Ridge was there, at least a Rivamonte, and Lake Garda, of course, and what he called Cividole, which seems to be Cividale del Friuli, near Venice, where he rested up.

Names change; phonetic spellings or spellings influenced by someone's primary foreign language—in my father's case, French—will make for difficulties in relocating the places thus misspelled. But I had not been merely seeking places in a calm professional hunt, I have to say. That panic was about losing more than my way. I *was*, at least in those bad moments in the troubled couple of hours in the library, searching for him. I am sure of it. Finger unsteady above the green and brown and purple pages that represented the landscape he had battled and finally bled in, my mouth so dry that I clacked when I pretended to my friends that I was having a *whale* of a time doing research for my clever bit of prose, I was searching for the man: *Where are you?* I was saying as I worked. *Where* are *you?*

When I write, then, when I place my characters in a geography I labor to make actual-feeling, in some way true, perhaps I'm trying to earn my reader's approval. Maybe I have to find him first. Maybe, when I write, I'm mapping him.

THE CHILDREN IN THE WOODS

I CALLED MY new and selected stories *The Children in the Woods* before I noticed, rereading *Bleak House*, that Dickens referred to "the children in the wood." He meant both Hansel and Gretel *and* his orphaned characters. I, too, referred to Hansel and Gretel. I, too, apparently, thought of my own characters in terms of them. And I must wonder why. Did I also think of my characters as somehow orphaned—deliberately lost in the dark, ferocious woods, to die of exposure or to be eaten, in order that their parents survive?

In this selection of stories, I included "My Father, Cont.," which is about a father who gets his family (himself included) lost in the snowy woods. They all survive, and the father does the Dagwood and Blondie thing: He parades his stubbornness, against the best advice of wife and family, and they all get to think, Oh, Daddy's gone and done it a-gain. But the story's more serious than that. The marriage is cracking and the child (who narrates it as an adult recollecting these events) is aware of menace in the forest and in their lives.

He says that he was

> *looking at the horrible illustrations in* Hansel and Gretel. *It's the story about the family with too little to eat. They kept taking the kids into the forest and leaving them there because there wasn't enough to go around. It's the saddest story about families. It's the one that says hunger comes first.*

So, I presume, I was thinking while I worked on the story that this child, well-enough loved, as he clearly is, might just be frightened enough by the fairy tale for his subconscious to suggest that his parents are taking him into the woods to leave him there "because there wasn't enough to go around." Notice that I didn't write "enough food": I was evidently thinking of more than food that was in short supply. I'm pleased that I didn't name it "love" or "need" or "assurance" or "affection": I'm pleased that I understood the Grimm story well enough— according to my understanding of it today—to see that, locked as it is into middle-class needs (food, money, firewood, and the sex or amity that might be Mrs. Woodcutter's handle on the father in the tale), the story is about more than food. As the boy in the story senses, it is *appetite* that galvanizes this family.

Looking backward, I move now from the story that I wrote in 1976 to what I might have been thinking of—the "Hansel and Gretel" with its "horrible illustrations," which leeched into my dreaming subconscious so long after I must have seen them. I was often given books of tales by my parents, and I disappeared into books of every sort at a very young age. But I know of only one copy of Grimm in our house, a proper home of the rising professional class in the Midwood section of Flatbush, in Brooklyn, New York, in the 1940s. The copy we own today comes from my wife's family and from the same time. I imagine that every other middle-class family in the United States bought a copy of the Grimm in February 1945, when it was offered, in its maroon binding, by the Book of the Month Club. (In December 1945, the Grimm and a green-bound Andersen were offered as a book dividend set by the club.)

I surely recall being attracted by Fritz Kredel's endpaper illustration for the Grimm: Handsome hunters, all of them looking now like second-rate cartoon figures drawn less capably than the Prince Valiant comic strip characters, bring home a slain dragon, his red tongue hanging down, his eyes closed in death beneath menacing eye sockets, his webby, clawed wings semierect; a king, an obedient queen, and a hot patootie princess who holds a laurel poised for presentation to the blond-maned hunter on a high white horse gather beneath a lemon or lime tree, and above them, on a hill, is an impossible Moorish castle.

It must have been the endpaper art of the Andersen that frightened me in the 1940s and 1950s. Arthur Szyk's teeming pages of fairy-tale figures—grimacing Chinese men; toys ready to move without warning; sad ballerinas; roots that clutch up like claws; dreamy Northern European children who grip menacing dolls; weeping ducks; and a wise-looking old man with a book on his lap, the words of which I now see are Szyk's love message to his family and to Denmark. I shied, I remember, from the interesting work of Szyk and cleaved to the banalities of Kredel.

Kredel's two pictures for "Hansel and Gretel" are about as unhorrible as can be—surely they're less menacing than the Rackham ones I find in the Opies' fairy tales, or the Sendak ones in the Randall Jarrell–Lore Segal *The Juniper Tree*. In one by Szyk, a parody of Miss Myrtle, my fifth-grade teacher, beckons smilingly from a tiny house "made of bread and roofed with cake." This witch is far less frightening than the long-nosed, rather bald woman who was determined that I not progress to grade six.

The picture that precedes the story itself, in brown ink on the wartime paper now growing tan, is a line drawing of several trees, before which two children stand together. Gretel, smaller than Hansel, leans on his chest and weeps. He embraces her, and his face, as he comforts her, suggests benevolent calm. They're both barefoot. And I know, as I study the illustration, that it is this drawing that returned over twenty-five or thirty years, that climbed up my spine and through the back door of my brain and out my fingers onto the keys of a typewriter in 1976. What called itself "horrible" is about vulnerability, enforced solitude, the condition of abandonment that must be among a child's greatest fears.

As I write these words, I recall telling my agent some years ago that I'd been thinking about a novel I proposed to write. In it, parents would love each other more than they could love the child they did indeed love. What would happen, I wondered, to the child—and how could the parents deal with the truth of their emotions? Of course, I was thinking of a variation of "Hansel and Gretel," I realize.

In the 1990s, I was drawn again by the story. I reread it. I thought about it. And I began to write stories in response to it. The stories were replies, I suppose, to the original story and to the interior self that kept returning to the first part of "Hansel and Gretel"—the part in which a mother convinces a father that they should abandon their children to the creatures of the forest so that the parents might survive. The latter part of the story—how the children outwit the witch and return to their loving father, his wife now dead, with the witch's gold—didn't interest me as a child and is only of interest now as one more upwardly mobile peasant's fairy tale: how we all lived happily ever after and didn't need to have jobs.

But it was the *bad* news I dwelled upon. I wrote half a dozen stories. Some of them, on revision, lost most visible connections to "Hansel and Gretel," but there surely was a good deal about the deceptions of parents in the first several drafts, and much of that, including any hint that Hansel ever dropped a trail of bread crumbs, has been revised away: The characters were stronger than my idea.

Many of those stories, on the other hand, continue to contain direct references to the fairy tale. There is one, "Bread," that refers directly, and in ways that please me, to the Grimm story. Another, a long story called "Berceuse"—the title is the French for "cradlesong"—concerns a New York intellectual named Miriam, who is in love with Sonny, husband of the narrator (a young woman named Kim); the story contains this dinner conversation:

> *Miriam was going to review a study of fairy tales, she said. Here it comes, I thought. She was going to surprise a few people, going to say a few things. "Believe me," she said. "For example, the Munich thing." She waved her fork at my marinated lamb without tasting it, enchanted as she was by my husband and herself.*
>
> *"The book fair?" Sonny dutifully asked. He twirled his knife like a baton. Often, at long dinners, he twirled his flatware and silently craved cigarettes.*
>
> *"Exhibition, they called it. I don't know German, the German word for it. I wouldn't know German. But yes: the fair, let's say. The authorities were quite horrified when several handsome editions of Hansel and Gretel were offered."*
>
> *Here it came. I said, "What's wrong with Hansel and Gretel?"*

"After the War?" she asked triumphantly.

Sonny said, "No. I don't get it either."

Miriam sighed through her nose. I had visions of jet black nostril hair, dense as scouring pads. "Do you remember the story?"

Sonny said, "Wicked stepmother, a father, they take the kids into the forest. They lose them. The kid leaves bread crumbs to follow back home, but birds eat the bread, the kids—"

"Something with a witch," I said, looking at Miriam.

"Right," Sonny said, twirling his knife, "the witch in the gingerbread house. She wants to eat the kids. No—the boy. Right? Maybe both of them. I forget. His sister helps him with something. I don't remember what. And they get home, with money, I think."

"Gold," Miriam said. "Of course. It's German. It's bourgeois, so of course *it celebrates money.* Looted money. But you're forgetting how *the witch wants to cook the boy."*

"In a big kettle," I said, envisioning a vast black kettle in a children's cartoon I had seen on TV one Saturday morning. I now saw Miriam in it, up to her neck in greasy liquid, a fricassee of harridan. "A giant cauldron of a kettle," I said.

Miriam looked pleased. "Oh, no, dears. In an oven. Ovens? Right after the War?"

"The Jews," I said, as if I'd just discovered them. "In Auschwitz. The ovens."

"The ovens," Miriam said. She added, "Good, Kim." Then, not waiting for me to wag my tail and pant, she said, "The German ovens. The reminder made the German bibliophiles a little uncomfortable. Ovens." Miriam smiled as if she had tasted something wonderful. I knew it wasn't on her plate.

All of these stories, one way or another, were about abandonment. One, called "Privacy," about a mother who left her husband and child—the husband, in turn, left the child with his inlaws so he could pursue his wife—went on for twenty pages and simply didn't work. I was talking about it with the novelist Richard Bausch as we sat in my car on the Colgate campus before he appeared in my classroom, in a course called Living Writers, to be interviewed by my students. His eyes widened. He shouted at me, "That's a fuckin' *novel!*" And he insisted. And it did became my novel *Long Way from Home.*

I stalled before committing myself to the toiling on that novel by worrying at the work my characters did. They all need to work, these fictive people, and I am incapable of getting on with a story or novel until I know my characters' vocations— the point at which their private selves touch the public world in any concentrated way. I swot up on vocations before I start a book, and I've learned a bit about plumbing and carpentry, medicine, wartime radio research, public school guidance and administration, being a policeman, delivering draft dodgers to Canada and delivering their mail to the States.

But that's the work the characters do. It isn't the story. And even though there are multiplicities of variation of story—of what Faulkner called "the problems of the human heart in conflict with itself"—there are very, very few subjects that we address that matter enough to us to be striven for as serious art. It costs too much to write. We don't do that work unless it matters in the bone. And, of all the imaginings available to us, we return to what matters the most. And I seem to return to the family unit as it frays and picks at itself, as it breaks or, sometimes, does not.

And the story of the mommy who knows the arithmetic of the household—how many may live, how many die, given what is left and what's in short supply—and of the daddy who says, in one translation, "Oh, I shall regret the poor children," and, in another, "But I grieve over the poor children"—this story strikes me as something of a very deep myth we tell one another, in different forms, over and over again.

Many of my students don't read fairy tales. Many cannot recall hearing fairy tales read to them. When I ask a seminar of seniors studying Dickens who "the children in the wood" might be, they cannot say. Nevertheless, they can read *Bleak House* with intelligence and can profit from it considerably. If they chose to read my fiction, they could maybe do the same. But they will not feel the vibration a reader of fairy tales from childhood could detect—that cello note resonating in the wood of the instrument and in the wood of the concert hall, or along the floor and furniture of a house, and on the skin of the listener. Reading now a work that is somehow agitated by this old story of children thrown away by their parents, one feels the unnameable emotion that Dickens—kept away at eleven or twelve, in a frightening London, from the rest of his family— felt as first a child and then as a writing adult. And I feel something like that from him, and felt it, apparently, before I knew about or read him, during the years I was certain that he wrote essentially about living happily ever after.

Fiction that matters, of course, cannot be about living happily ever after. Serious writers don't, I think, believe in it— although they might keep wanting to. Serious writing is about the trail of lifesaving bread crumbs that are eaten by the forest birds. It is about being disposable. It is about what you say to yourself even if you have defeated the terrible darkness of nighttime in the forest, or the witch and her oven, or the dangerous, unmapped distance that separates you from home. It is about living with a truth you've discerned but don't want to know. It is about hunger, how hunger comes first.

FOR THE LOVE OF
A PRINCESS OF MARS

꽃꽃꽃

IT'S PAST ELEVEN on a Friday night in the spring of 1955.
Here comes a kid down the length of Eighteenth Street in the
Midwood section of Flatbush, in Brooklyn, New York. He
passes the kempt lawns and tidy hedges under big leafy
sycamores and maples. The middle class is asleep, and most of
the houses attached to the lawns are dark, though an occasional
window pulses with blue-gray television light. Streetlamps
shine benignly, and Mars is red in the sky. The kid is on his way
home from the weekly meeting of Troop 8, Boy Scouts of
America, which convenes on the top floor of a large church and
meetinghouse, the Flatbush-Tompkins Congregational. There,
the boys march raggedly on the undersized basketball court,
tie bandages on one another's healthy limbs, stop make-believe
arterial bleeding, and slam basketballs at one another with the
accurate cruelty of the very young.

This kid is no less vicious in dodgeball, and no less dedicated to the imprecise precision marching, the saluting, and other paramilitary pleasures. But he also knows that he will soon enough be alone, walking with nobody else from Dorchester Road, past Ditmas, Newkirk, Foster, toward Avenue I and home and, in a sleeping house, a room with no one in it.

The solitude is some of the point: the skies full of stars above the low buildings, the silence on the curving Avenue H bridge above the electric wires and the Long Island Railroad tracks. But much of the anticipation and pleasure in that solitary walk is what makes the chubby kid—in his kneesocks and khaki shorts and a shirtful of badges won for miscooking meat and firing a .22 and humping a heavy knapsack on long hikes—lean awkwardly and duck his chin against his bright neckerchief and pause to readjust the heavy load that is so far from being a burden.

He is carrying books. He is a pretty decent athlete who can hit a pink Spaulding with a broomstick and thump around with some effect in football games. But he is also always moving away from these congregations and cooperations. He pines for company yet wishes to be alone. He Boy Scouts for the hugger-mugger of the troop, and also because they have made him the troop librarian. He gets to check the books out, so a little power lies for him among the tattered cards, the red-inked date stamp, the authority of issuing what to him is so important. But he also gets to hoard those books for himself, a Scrooge among books, since so few besides he take them out.

So, every Friday night, he carries home a stack of six or seven books. He reads them late, he wakes early on Saturday to read—under the green light through the high leafy trees in the yards on Eighteenth Street—and he reads as he brushes his teeth, as he eats his breakfast, reads until his foot hits the front-door threshold and his entrance into the world of stickball, or a Boy Scout trip, or the part-time job in the pharmacy, where

he dusts off dull wares, paying close, confused attention to the
mystery of condoms.

SOME OF THE books were published by Saalfield, apparently
owned by Crown: *Dave Dawson at Singapore, Dave Dawson,
Flight Lieutenant,* stories of World War II. Some were from
Cupples & Leon: Noel Sainsbury's Great Ace Series, titles like
Billy Smith—Secret Service Ace, published in the late twenties.
But most of the irresistible ones were published by Grosset &
Dunlap, with their fibrous red cloth covers and yellowing paper
that, at the corners of the page, turned brown and chipped away
as the page was turned. These were from the thirties. The later
editions, in tan and grainy bindings, were published in the forties in Tarzana, California. Their titles instantly recall for me
my being that kid, those long anticipatory walks of a Friday
night, the falling upon and into and through the pages in the
alien worlds of Edgar Rice Burroughs: *Pirates of Venus, Tarzan
Triumphant, Maid of Mars,* and, the ur-Burroughs for me, *A
Princess of Mars.*

For, while I admired Tarzan's socially acceptable savagery,
his courage and strength, and his ability to wear a loincloth
with panache while swinging through trees and carrying a dishy
woman—his careering in dinner dress through the posher ar-
rondissements of Paris was my favorite—the Martian adventures won my heart and kept me up the latest.

Princess begins, like many more literary works—think of *The
Scarlet Letter* or *Gulliver's Travels*—in disguise. The wily author
says, in effect, Here is an actual piece of recorded history; you
can believe it; it is *fact;* I have seen the pages with my own eyes.

Edgar Rice Burroughs, speaking, he says, "very sincerely,"
offers us, in his introduction, a favor. He says he's "submitting
Captain Carter's strange manuscript to you in book form." It's
not make-believe, see? It's the truth, and he vouches for it. He

recalls for us the author of the factual memoir we're to read. He is a man of "hearty good fellowship," whom "we all loved." Why, "our slaves fairly worshipped the ground he trod." And I never winced—I, the budding egalitarian, the child of registered Democrats. Well, he *was*, after all, "a splendid specimen of manhood . . . broad of shoulder and narrow of hip," and "His manners were perfect, and his courtliness was that of a typical southern gentleman of the highest type." How, then, could I resist?

I realize now, of course, that I, with my greasy forehead and six-inch pompadour permanently erect, with my manhood specimen registering narrow of shoulder and broad of hip, wanted to *be* John Carter. Throw in the frontispiece by Frank Schoonover, and I was lost: That glossy page shows John Carter (who looks a little thin in the thigh to me, these days, and whose arms seem stringy) in battle. His gear is leathery, big, full of gadgets and gimmicks and bulk and heft, a siren song for space-opera dreamers such as I. His huge pistols bulge from swollen holsters, his long, thin sword looks as ceremonial as it looks wicked. The caption: "With my back against a golden throne, I fought once more for Dejah Thoris."

And there, behind him, curved and slinky, a dream of bare shoulders and long arms and a Cleopatra hairdo, crouches Dejah Thoris, the Princess of Mars. Guns, sex, broadness of shoulder, narrowness of hip: What else could a boy—a kid who hangs by his fingertips above the Abyss of Adolescence—ask for?

This: that John Carter, cordial among slaves and courtly with women, was *moody*. John Carter was like me! For he often would "sit for hours gazing off into space," it says in the introduction. Did I learn from this single book all of the clichés I must as a writer avoid? I surely didn't register them at the time. In Carter's face, according to this introduction to a real manuscript by an actual person as reported by this estimable author, was "a look of wistful longing and hopeless misery." He looked "up into the heavens." Later, telling Mr. Burroughs that "if anything should happen to him," he was to use a certain key to open a certain compartment in his safe, John Carter is found dead. In the safe are instructions, and a manuscript. Dutifully, Mr. Burroughs waits twenty-one years to examine its pages— which now lie before me.

So there I went, into its pages, to find out how our hero died—though I was certain he really hadn't. Death, at twelve, and thirteen, and fourteen, was a mistake on the part of the grown-ups. I read of an exciting battle, a cave in the Arizona hills in 1866, and how Carter, thinking himself about to die, finds his attention drawn to the "large red star . . . Mars, the god of war . . . for me, the fighting man, it had always held the power of irresistible enchantment."

Drawn by the verisimilitude of the beginning, agog to read about a man who was in all ways superior where I found myself deficient, and acknowledging that I, too, had always been drawn by Mars in the night sky, since its color made it the only celestial object I could identify, I read on.

Carter gazes at Mars. It draws him—how else?—"as the lodestone attracts a particle of iron." There is "an instant of extreme cold and utter darkness," and John Carter wakes to find himself on Mars, among ten-legged waddling creatures the size of Shetland ponies, with jaws that have three rows of tusks, and among beings with names like Tars Tarkas and Sola—she is eight feet tall, a light olive green, and is quite sweet—and of course there is Dejah Thoris, Princess of Helium, daughter of Mars.

There was Tarzan; there was Cheetah; there was Jane. There was *At the Earth's Core* and *Pellucidar*, its sequel. They were as exciting as the adventures of Carson Napier in the *Venus* series. But of all Burroughs's creations, the ones I loved most were the novels in the *Mars* series: *The Warlord of Mars, A Fight-*

ing Man of Mars, the story of *Thuvia, a Maid of Mars*. And it all had begun with the *Princess*.

As I reexamine the books, I cannot find one original tactic of storytelling, one authentic invention of prose. It is all cowboys and Indians; it contains every convention of adventure writing perfected in the nineteenth century and repeated in the films starring everyone adored in the 1940s. Handsome women respond to handsome men in this fashion: "A pretty flush overspread her face. . . ." And fighting men thus pitch their woo: "I ask you, my princess, to be mine." She places her "dear hands" on his shoulders and so, reader, "I took her in my arms and kissed her."

And I loved it. My wars were fought by surrogates. My mistresses were little, adoring, and no more threatening than Jean Arthur or Myrna Loy.

I learn now that *A Princess of Mars* was among Burroughs's first sales. With a shorter, different foreword note, under the splendid pen name Norman Bean, it was serialized as *Under the Moons of Mars* in *The All-Story* magazine in 1912. In a recent study, a critic makes the case that the novel is actually informed by the mythic katabasis—death and descent into the underworld—and he's probably right. So, either I, with my sad complexion, my merit badges, and my late-night longings, was being mythic and katabasic or something else was afoot on the crimson sands of Mars.

I suspect it was simply the reveling in the adventures of someone larger, stronger, braver, and more capable than I. Surely that delight must be some of what draws me to study a great football player in full charge, as he sees events on the field in slow motion as he plays with a ferocity I can only dream of exerting on the physical world.

And I suspect it was the innocent sexuality of the books. Dejah Thoris was chaste, unreachable, and so was every girl I loved, of the many I was always in love with—unreachable by *me*. Sex may have, at last, been the compelling force of the novels, the engine that made their cumbersome, clanking machinery go. It showed no breasts, required no confrontations of flesh (except in war), and was not finally about the limbs and loins of Dejah Thoris; it was about her unseizable beauty, her abstract glamour. For me, therefore, she was safe: I didn't need to know any mechanics and could keep my boxer shorts on. She was the other side of what pitched me, not very long afterward, onto the BMT subway, over the East River, to the Eighth Street Bookshop, where I would buy and smuggle home the Modern Library *Ulysses* because I had heard that Mr. Joyce was a dirty writer. Molly Bloom became my sweaty fantasy, but Dejah Thoris was my dream girl.

I later found aspects of her in Rider Haggard's *She*, in Lionel Davidson's *The Rose of Tibet*, in the sad, bad temptresses of Raymond Chandler. Some of her is in Le Carré's Ann, Smiley's beautiful, faithless, yet somehow innocent wife. In these later works, she is some of Molly Bloom; but first, in the early conceptions of the man who loves and loses her, she is some of Dejah Thoris: abstractly beautiful, appealing most to the mind, born of an exotic world, too high in station to hope for, but someone for whom it is compellingly necessary to fight and conceivably die. She is the romantic dream. She lives in the minds of boys. And every man who writes is partly a boy. And so is every man who doesn't.

We do not, of course, witness the consummation of John Carter's love for Dejah Thoris. We do, however, see the "golden incubator" in which reposes their "snow-white egg." We speak of interspecies love, of course—as do, in fact, all immature boys who dream of an enchanted coupling with flesh-and-blood women. Not a day passed, we are told—when, of course, Carter is home from his incessant battles as warlord in the armies of Helium and "a prince of the house of Tardo Mors"—that "Dejah Thoris and I [did not] stand hand in hand before our little shrine planning for the future, when the delicate shell would break."

Now, *there* is a consequence of barely imaginable sexual congress that a kid *can* get next to: He stands not only outside the egg, in Carter's big shoulders, holding hands with a gorgeous princess; he is also *in* the egg, this kid, waiting to break through into what he can hardly dream will be the real, grown-up life of achievement for which he waits.

I am celebrating six feet, two inches of gentleman soldier who can sail his battleship through the thin air of Mars using the Barsoomian Eighth Ray, and who, in a fight with something large and many-legged, can close "my fingers, vise-like, upon its windpipe."

I am celebrating a princess who, with "dilated eyes and quickening breath, and then with an odd little laugh, which brought roguish dimples to the corner of her mouth," can cry, " 'What a child! A great warrior and yet a stumbling little child.' "

That's me, Dejah Thoris. Be a mommy *and* a lover: Have my egg *and* hatch me in it. And *katabasis* me no *katabasis*. The truth about myths, death, descent, and the news of the world will all have their day, and soon enough. Meanwhile, however, through John Carter's eyes, "I can see, across the awful abyss of space, a beautiful black-haired woman standing in the garden of a palace." John Carter, through the whimsy of the mechanics of space travel, has been sent back to Earth, where he conducts his awful exile with gracefulness to the slaves. He waits to return to his impossibly beautiful woman, as I waited for the appearance of mine.

Beside Dejah Thoris is their child, now hatched, for whom "she points into the sky toward the planet Earth, while at their feet is a huge and hideous creature with a heart of gold." I lived his impossible longing, perhaps sensing that it was a condition ushered into a boy's life by the enfleshment of his romantic prayers.

But I had my hopes. I could say, with John Carter, "I believe that they are waiting there for me. . . ." I was the lover, I was the child, and I was beginning to learn that it was desirable to know how to cause a stranger to dream such dreams as those of John Carter and me.

A RELATIVE LIE

In MARCH 1991, I began a story that I at last wrote well or well enough, and nevertheless failed to write as I had wanted to or needed to and, more important, as it should have been written. Writing a story is like climbing a rock face that has few handholds; you have to find leverage for fingers and toes, and you have to be able to focus a great deal of strength through small muscles, holding on, pushing up while leaning out, almost as if you were lying on the surface of the sea and trusting it not to take you under, and using your experience and intuition at once—doing what you know well while discovering as you do it how to work new surfaces.

This is about a story the material of which I knew rather well, but the treatment of which—like a powdering, dangerous pitch—I hadn't ever attempted. I thought I knew what I wanted to do, and, after awhile, I felt certain of where I was going. I finished the story, and it was published in a good-enough magazine, from the editor of which it received ample editing. I reprinted it in *The Children in the Woods*, my new and selected stories of 1994, and a number of readers said they admired it. Yet I knew that the story, "Folk Tales," was a failure.

It is true that, hanging by my fingertips, working my way into this crevice and onto that small ledge, I had found a story I could manage to tell that represented some good part of what I thought I had set out to tell. I didn't fall to my death, I suppose. But I'm not certain how far and how commendably— with what courage or vision—I climbed. Perhaps how I failed is how some other writers fail and, by extension, how nonwriters—who also need to tell the stories in their lives for the sake of some kind of health and who sometimes rely on people like me to do it on their behalf—can "succeed" at how and what they tell while knowing that they have failed themselves and the matter they have tried to narrate.

I have said that I didn't write the story as it should have been written. By that *should*, I mean the amalgam of lived or observed or otherwise-historical events and facts that prod the writer, providing him with a need to find narrative and metaphors by which the essence of that amalgam feels (to the writer) honestly served and the reader intelligently entertained. It is my contention that good stories matter critically to the reader, and that the writer is instructed by no smaller injunction than David Copperfield's, as he starts the story of his life (and his becoming a writer) by saying—by challenging himself— "Whether I shall turn out to be the hero of my own life, or whether that station will be held by anybody else, these pages must show."

In the case of which I'm speaking, the successful failure of the story "Folk Tales," I begin with a rainy day in 1949. I was in the kitchen of our home on East Eighteenth Street in the

Midwood section of Flatbush, a neighborhood of three-story homes that were built a few years after the turn of the century. Our kitchen had a linoleum floor embossed with a pattern of red brick imitative of what you might find in a patio behind one of these homes. I sat at the shiny blue Formica table that seemed then to be long and wide, and I designed an atomic bomb.

I was eight and a half years old and almost bored, though reading about or drawing the appurtenances of the future as defined by warfare was never uninteresting to me. I had little artistic talent, but I loved to draw. I appreciated the smells I associated with what in the first grade we called "art"— the vanilla of coarse tan construction paper, the harsh waxiness of crayon, the vinegary compost of library paste. In the kitchen, on a rainy Saturday afternoon, with nothing to do, and doubtless goaded by science-fiction magazines and stories of space exploration and fictive heroes of the recently concluded war, I made love to my imagination and war upon the world.

I drew the bomb and the plane that dropped it. I wrote to Albert Einstein about my little piece of the apocalypse:

> *Carrying in the nose a long piece of plastic about a foot long and one inch wide resting against the back of one atom, and another atom two feet away, both of the atoms are on a rack. The rocket is carried in the bom bay of a B-36. When released over enemy teratory it hurtles tword ground at a fast speed. Thus if it is discovered by a lookout of the russain ground crew it can go into use before anything can be done about it. When the rocket hits ground the peice of plastic which is strikeing out propells the lower atom tword the higher atom. When the lower atom reaches the higher atom, the big exploisen comes.*

P.S. This is only in case of war, believe me I do not want war!

FREDERICK M. BUSCH Age 8 1/2

P.S. Unemployed.

I must have read the "Unemployed" in an adventure story about a soldier or soldier of fortune who felt underutilized. I cannot account for the inconsistency in my misspelling of the word *piece*, nor do I understand why I, whose knowledge of the *Dave Dawson* World War II series by R. Sidney Bowen was complete, could not spell *bomb bay*. How come I knew *hurtles* but not *explosion?* I can, of course, see the crooked heart and dark mind behind the first postscript. I didn't want war, eh? What piety. What early fiction from the smiler with the bomb.

I could not type at eight and a half, I think—surely not well enough to ready a letter for Einstein. And I suspect that even I—who would show off his cuteness in the middle of a house fire, who would lie for the sake of invention itself to the firemen seeking directions to the burning house—*might* not have thought to type the letter and send it off. So perhaps I will submit to my desire to blame the arrogant submission of this weapon to end all weapons on my proud and loving parents. And, surely, the typewriter's signatures—certain crooked characters—on the carbon copy of my letter are identical to those found on other documents pounded into being on the giant boxy Underwood by Miss Bertha Schwab, my father's dedicated secretary at the law firm of Katz & Sommerich. I believe that it was my parents who found out where to send my plans. But I know that it was I, a writer even then, I think, who somehow provoked them, beaming agents, to mail off my designs. Though never really lost, I was always intent on being found.

I sent the plans to Einstein either because my parents thought I ought to or because I had seen his pictures in *Life* and, I remember, I thought he was nice and had a patient smile. Like me, according to *Life*, he forgot assignments and errands. He wore sweatshirts, as kids did. He was the smartest man in the history of the universe. And it was raining that Saturday and nobody was playing stickball in the street.

My father mailed my letter and drawing from his law offices, and Einstein answered. My memory of his response is difficult to vouch for. I heard my parents, usually my mother, tell the story a lot, and I no longer know whether I remember what happened or what the world was told had happened. Here are the events as recalled or constructed.

The mail arrives one day, and it is pointed out to me that I have a letter from Princeton, New Jersey. The envelope containing it is yellowing now; it is roughly six and three-quarters inches by three and three-quarters inches, and it bears a purple three-cent stamp. It is addressed "Frederic K. M. Bush 956 East 18.Str. Brooklyn 30, New York." Each period doubles itself, as if it were a colon and what ought to be a full stop is here a sign of more to come. The "Str." is for *Strasse*, yes?

The return address on the envelope says "112 Murcer Str. Princeton, N.J." The embossed letterhead declines to the right in small increments: *A. Einstein*, and then *112 Murcer Street*, then *Princeton*, then *New Jersey, U.S.A.*

Since Miss Schwab typed my full name at the bottom of the letter, and since Einstein's reply (dated "4 April, 1950") is headed "Dear Freddy," I wonder whether I signed that name or whether a parent told a genius what a genius he or she was parent to. Here is what the actual genius replied:

> *I received your letter of March 31st, and regret it very much that such a young person should be already interested*

> *in such ugly purposes as military inventions. Kindness and*
> *understanding is much more important.*
>
> Yours sincerely,
> Albert Einstein.

I was told again and again of what followed. The war baby invented his darling bomb and he received instead of thanks and praise a bombshell: I was told, and dinner guests were told, and after awhile we all told one another. I came to hear it and see it and feel it—the glass and wood and iron of the high, heavy Art Deco door at the front of the Brooklyn house, and the parquet floor on which I writhed with early rejection, *crumpling Einstein's letter*: the April fool, the writer scorned.

"He stole my invention!" I was told I cried. (I believe, in fact, that he did not return the original letter I sent, nor the all-important crayon drawings on construction paper.) "He stole my invention!"

And there, then, that night, near the Art Deco door, on the parquet floor—why there?—my mother erected her ironing board. And there she stood—there, in the story, forever young and ever serving, she stands: It is my mother, patiently ironing flat the letter to her son from Albert Einstein, pressing it, stroke after stroke, back to its innocence, and back to his.

I was told for years about the letters to and from Princeton, but I wasn't shown them. My parents wouldn't risk my seizing the letter, they said, and selling it. My wife, Judy, and I, on Morton Street in Greenwich Village in 1963, were impressively poor and always in a financial crisis. Spam sustained us, tuna was a luxury; I would have sold that letter if I could. But when the danger was deemed to be past, when I was in my thirties (though really no more solvent), I had the documents. We looked them over and discussed my clever, cute intelligence and placed them in our safe-deposit box and never looked at them again until 1989, when we moved our belongings to a different bank.

Opening the envelope from Princeton for the third time in my life, I again felt rebuked: One always is, with luck, part child. Perhaps, too, I felt Einstein's severity as an adult should. How was he to know—"believe me I do not want war!"—that I spoke not of bombs, although they were a part of my consciousness in 1949, but of *invention*? My notions of death and the low and higher atom had, I think, to do with *me*, with what I could construct of ignorance and id and the imagination—and with demonstrating to Einstein and the rest of the adults how I flew through the air, how I landed with such grace. He wrote to me of sacred life; I read *rejection slip*.

I thought such thoughts as we looked at the letter in 1989. And then Judy, a librarian, who looks at words on paper and sees what the rest of us see, but who also sees *documents*, pointed this out: The letter isn't crumpled, and it never was. There are no jagged bendings or tears. The paper was never wounded. It bears no witness to distress, aside from its author's language. And, trying in 1989 to write about these events, I asked whose mythology one deals with—whose fiction—when reading the flat, unwrinkled, and sad generosity of Albert Einstein's letter to a kid, feeling nifty, who sought to be praised for his gift of death.

I made a pun, then, about the relativity of truth, and I stopped my speculations there, failing for the first time—the story I tried to write marked the second—to climb what was clearly a challenging pitch: Why had my mother lied? And why had she sustained the lie?

In 1991, I wrote a story based on these events—triggered by them, I suppose I should say, or detonated, at last, on a very long fuse. The first draft was called "Folk Art," which became "Folk Tales," and which was published in *Story* in the winter of 1992. It tells about and is narrated by Howie, an analyst, like his author a child of Brooklyn, who (unlike his author) is separated from his wife and living in a sublet apartment in Manhattan. An uncle, Bernie, whom he hasn't seen for years, comes to call. Howie is flooded with guilt, for this is his mother's brother, and Howie has avoided contact. His uncle brings a safe-deposit key he promised Howie's mother he would keep for his nephew. But the uncle is off for Houston, for tricky heart surgery, and, unsure that he'll survive, he thinks it wise to at least give Howie the key. What is in the safe-deposit box, he suggests, is supposed to change Howie's life. So it is a kind of folk or fairy tale, concerning transformations that we seek and that we come to fear we might deserve. On a sentimental journey to Brooklyn, Howie realizes that he loves his uncle and has failed him; I wonder, as I write this, whether affection for the uncle was a surrogate emotion for the mother, whose double the uncle might be. I knew no such uncle, by the way, and I loved inventing him. He told stories, in my story, about my grandfather Buschlowitz, who remembered the cossacks and the pogroms, and who, like the grandfather in the story, did indeed drive a rabbi from his apartment, spitting at him, long before his children in America changed his name.

In the box, at the Dime Savings Bank of Brooklyn, where our family did its local banking in the 1940s and 1950s, Howie finds the reply to a letter he now remembers writing to Albert Einstein. He recalls that he had crumpled it and that his mother had ironed it back to smoothness. The discovery of the letter creates in Howie the need to tell his rediscovered story—rainy day, bomb, Einstein, et cetera. But he is without a wife who loves him and would listen, and his uncle is by now in Houston, maybe dead. Howie is alone. His work requires that he listen to the stories of others, not tell them his. So he, a listener in what Freud's patient called "the talking cure," can't talk. He is condemned not to tell his story, and the story, "Folk Tales," ends.

The crucial fact, my mother's fiction, among so many other facts, was in my memory and at the front of my mind as I wrote the little essay called "The Higher Atom," and then the story called "Folk Art," and then its successor, "Folk Tales," rewritten four or five times, then edited and seen through publication and into public reception—examined, probed, revised, and honed every time—as the story of what my character received as powerful metaphoric truth and which is, of course, in the life and in the art, a lie.

It seemed, that gradual loss of what had started the story off for me, to be part of the usual process of feeling one's way toward the story's reality. The art of it, the toning down into the softer and contemplative ending of the story, did seem to prevent my writing a sudden denunciation or discovery of the mother's fiction. Yet the story had been born and had seemed to exist for that discovery's sake. Instead of the mother being a memory, a set of loving obligations and reminiscences in an uncle's mouth—he speaks the history the son has sublimated— she, if the story was to be true to its background, its authorial impulses, what I earlier called "its essence," would have to be evoked early on in "Folk Tales." Her lies would, I thought and still think, have to be seen as suspect—ultimately, in some sense, duplicitous.

Which raises, of course, the problem of structure: One would have to build into early moments of the story some aspect of the mother as a presence—not the absence she powerfully is in the finished version—and then, like a bomb that really works, her infidelity to actual events would have to explode upon the protagonist and the reader. The narrator, then, and his author, too, would have to deal with, among other thoughts and feelings, the question of the relationship of lived moments to the recitation of history, the question of whether a fiction is a lie and of whether an artful lie may not be true—

and, naturally, the question of the value and measurement of what we call "truths."

There is also the problem of modulation. Is the mother sublimated by Howie because she is in other ways treacherous? Is she treacherous only in this singular, antiromantic way? How much of her, in the form of memories and the uncle's recollections during his one brief visit to Howie and to the surface of the story itself, would have to be summoned in some dramatic way?

I see the writer on those ledges and edges I have spoken about. He is feeling his way up and into the story. Spurred into this dangerous venture by the story of the mother's story, he makes his decisions, invokes his expertise, lunges into risk, lies back against the empty air, not quite falling, and he makes the top—he completes the story—by avoiding the very element that made him, in the first place, start this climb.

He *seems* both safe and achieved. The story is done, and people seem to like it. Yet he knows that he has failed to do what he set out to do. And he values being a writer in part because of its risks and because he sees himself as trying to be honest in spite of—because of?—those risks. So does he, really, have a finished story if it isn't what he meant to do?

Of course he does.

But it isn't the story he thinks he should have written. And he lives by injunctions—*should have*—and perhaps he writes to earn his sense of merit or grace. So he feels unworthy. (What a pity he can't visit Howie's office and tell *him*. But of course that's what he might have tried to do by attempting the story.)

So does the writer have to live with a kind of wound caused by his having avoided the story's great risks? Of course he does. For the risks in (and to) the story are not only structural, although I have possibly made them seem to be. What's important is that I haven't developed the source of Howie's avoidance of his family's history and of his mother's surrogate, the uncle.

And I haven't confronted *my* avoidance of my mother's history, which is, as I have shown, the trigger for my writing the story in the first place.

The more I think of the story, and I seem to need to think of it, the more I believe that it fails by not facing the wonderful lie Howie's mother offers her son as legacy. Howie can face it from his place in his mother's future. But he doesn't. And I suspect that I made him, finally, mute, because I knew—felt—that *I* was. I silenced my protagonist because I had shut up. He spoke, not speaking, for me.

To tell the story right, somehow, to tell it truly, I would have had to write a scene in which the mother tells Howie's wife, before their divorce, that the mother, through her actual genes, was the cause and sustainer of his gifts. I would have had to show her loving him pathologically, telling lies to herself and him and others until her history with her son belonged to her alone, because she had rewritten it—because her ardor was for herself, and she had, in making her fictions of him and her life with him, shaped him as her metaphor, if not precisely her mirrored self.

By effecting Howie's escape into her future, and by reducing her to words on paper—to an *absence* represented by a letter and a domestic myth—I of course made my own escape. I would not have to write the mother I didn't want to face. So I made the story work well enough without her. I responded to the inherent structure given to language and events by the mother and the uncle and Howie, I told myself. And maybe that is true.

And maybe it isn't; and maybe what I did was help my character sidestep what I wished not to face by building the story so that, for structure's sake, I was required, veteran craftsman, to sidestep the lie that is the story's basic truth.

And, if that is the case, then I lied.

So I have been—I am—a character in a lie. I live in somebody's fiction, you might want to say. And I am trying to tell you, and trying to tell myself, the truth, or some of it, about how a man examines a page of the text that his life, in one of its versions, seems to have become. He seizes it, he pulls it close, he breathes his breath upon it, and he reads it again and again. It has been, surely, violated. It also seems to be whole. He thinks it is both at once.

THE WRITER'S WIFE

I CANNOT SPEAK for writers' husbands because I have never been or loved one. But I live with a writer's wife, and I can tell you that the sentence of a writer's wife is commuted by nothing short of death. You have seen them, smiling in crowded gatherings at no one because no one talks to them for very long except to say, "Oh, you're Mrs. Him? How *wonderful!*" They say this as if she has balanced a ball on her nose or stolen Him from the women, student poets, who would nurse him in his powerful senility, or bake him cookies to crumble in a postgraduate bed. You have seen them, listening to Him read to strangers the story or poem or chapter or essay about his claim to have made long and tireless epiphanic love in a sweaty lather with a woman half her age but how it is *she* to whom he is true because of the metaphor his return to her makes it possible for him to write for them to hear while she sits among them and smiles while her face pulses and shines.

It isn't always that bad, of course. We all know writers' wives whose husbands are faithful. These are the fortunate women who can count on the fidelity with which their writer husband is going to tell them, every day, and often on the hour, how he feels—truly. He is going to report to her his fears and needs. When they were girl and boy, she knew at once that she was needed. He wooed her, you know, this faithful husband, this man who loves her more than his life (and as much as the present manuscript) with his words. They sat on the edge of the bed he could not coax her into during that first weekend together in Greenwich Village, five flights up over Charles Street, and he read her every story he had written. *Each one*, in order of composition, one after the other after the other. That was when she learned to keep her eyes wide in eager audition, as if she were about to learn the salient fact for which, her whole life, she had waited. *Feed me! Feed me!* her happily hungry face was learning to say.

He is reliable. He greets her at the door, or limps (as if the constantly twinging flesh wound of life were aggravated by the weather, or a committee meeting or seminar) from the car to the house, and he faithfully tells her of (a) how he wrote nothing good that day; (b) how the man or woman he went to graduate school with has won a MacArthur, the National Book Award, and/or the Pulitzer; (c) how his Ph.D.-bearing colleagues disdain him for being a barbarian; (d) how this wonderful student—she should see this woman, with hair the color of et cetera and breasts like so forth—"ripe as a goddamned *peach*," he tells his day-worn wife of ten or twenty or thirty years—has come to him in utter need, poor kid, she's so dependent on him, because . . . And, reliably, with fidelity to the facts and to his needs, he tells her something unessential, which ultimately pivots on the painful fact of someone's—could have been the student's, but it's going to end up his—deep needs.

This is the wife who, traveling with him and their lap-riding infants to foreign capitals, has heard out his fears that he'll never have the peace of mind—she's changing the diarrhea-drenched diaper on the airplane as the child, in the sixth hour of their journey, squirms and wails—to get his writing done. This is the wife who watches—who helps him push—as he moves the furniture about their rented flat so that he has a workroom. It is she who helps him find the rental offices, who encourages him to acquire the word processor they can't afford, because it is, after all, his *art*. This wife chased after a wandering two-year-old in the Lake District of England, a bag of rough yarn tied to her belt, as she knitted squares for a blanket she would use, she told her husband, as a shroud for either her or the kid—whoever succumbed first. He, meanwhile, had moved a desk into the largest room of their small stone house, the bathroom, and was writing a long story about something he had come—is there any doubt of this?—to feel with important urgency.

So he felt guilty. It took awhile, because the self is deep and the writer surfaces slowly from his long, dark dive. And guilt, like colds to parents and grade-school teachers, builds immunities; it takes awhile to understand you've caught it again. His soles are sticky with Kafka, he tracks Cheever on the floor, and he sups the broth of Roth; guilt is on the wind and in the air and in his sinuses, his lungs. But, after awhile, he understands that this soreness is his conscience, and he vows to change his ways.

Writers' wives are those women who not only receive the hourly report of shifts in the weather of the soul; they are the women to whom vows are made with as much frequency as to the wives of gamblers, alcoholics, drug addicts, and politicians.

This summer, he swears to her, he is not going to take his laptop on their vacation. They have planned to spend two weeks in the woods next to Cathance Lake, in Maine, where they will be close to friends they don't yet know they will lose forever, and where their two young boys can canoe and fish. They will rent a place at the isolated lake, and he will not write.

The writer's wife is the woman pretending—see the wide eyes, the deceptively casual smile—that she does not envision a nightmare of summertime fidelity: He is going, she knows, to report faithfully every nuance of each terror of withdrawal from his work; she is going to be the protagonist of a Harlequin Romance entitled *Nurse Muse at Hell Lake.* She encourages him to take along his laptop and spend their vacation bullying and whining about his work. Do it, darling. Do it for art. Do it for the National Book Awards Committee. Do it for the advance you will barely persuade your publisher to come across with and which you'll tell me, after signing the contract, is too small.

But he is set on selflessness, and he carries it out with the drama of a diva in decline. That would have been a good corner to write in, he suggests, pawing at the fishing rod wrapped in a tangle of line and lure he will ultimately deliver, like a bleeding limb, for her attention. This is great, he says, leading the boys out to the canoe from which, she is positive, he will spill her sons to drown. It's early and gorgeous, he tells her, and I'm not hidden inside writing at anything, I'm in the *world.* He discovers existence for her, and she can only—as she knows he needs her to—suggest that she take the boys while he writes. Not *this* trip, he says, adjusting his shirt to the multiple arrows embedded in his martyr's flesh.

And at night, on the screened-in porch, after seeing the boys in their beds, after some Irish whiskey and slow talk, they lie down to sleep. They are private, they are more in the woods than in the house here, and they listen to the loons call over the lake. And at dawn on the third day of vacation, she is wakened by his stiffening. No: not the happy, lazy lust of early morning. It is his entire body that is stiff. She opens her eyes reluctantly, for fear that she will see her husband's heart explode through his chest, or his mouth twist in a stroke-frozen joke about laughter.

His eyes are huge. His lips are compressed, as if in pain, as if—yes: rage. Her husband in his boxer shorts, in a screened-in porch at Cathance Lake, in Maine, is angry. Of course, he often is. There are totalitarians of Right and Left discoverable everywhere, and there are the usual editors bent on rejecting or demeaning his work, and there are all the men and women of America who are trying to silence him by never buying his books. This one, though, is a fragile anger—he's bewildered and outraged at once.

Responding to her motion, not moving his eyes—she sees them staring through the screen at the dense surrounding forest—he says to her, "Listen!"

She answers, "I don't hear anything."

"*Listen*, damn it."

She hears nothing for them to fear.

He closes his eyes, and his face is like a fist. He hisses, "*There*."

She shakes her head.

"Some son of a bitch," he tells her, "is out there someplace *typing*."

She listens harder, separating birdcall from squirrel squeak, wind through birches from the lake's slow slap on the stones of the shore. She hears it then, and she focuses through the other noises, brings it in. Her face twists into what she knows he will later resent aloud as a patronizing smile. She suppresses what she can. She pulls the covers over her face and tries to hide.

He names it again, the personal affront, his lifetime's disorder and salvation: "Who in hell is goddamn *typing* this time of the night?"

She has to. She says it hurriedly and under the muffling bedclothes, and she knows he's going to ask it.

"What?" he snarls.

So she comes up from under the blankets. "Woodpecker,"

she confesses. "Welcome to the woods. It's a woodpecker peck-
ing for bugs."

"It's a woodpecker?" he says. "It's a bird?"

It's your brain, she doesn't tell him.

He says, "It's a bird? Nobody's writing?"

"Nobody's writing," she assures him, though he is, she
knows.

THE FLOATING
CHRISTMAS TREE

It's all true: Greenwich Village, real poverty, heartbreak in the mails, and famous writers in coffeehouses on Sheridan Square—"That's Thomas Pynchon!" "Who's he?"—and now that some years are between me and those days and I can look on them squarely, I am required to report that little has changed. I no longer live in Greenwich Village, it is true, but in upstate New York; my poverty is, like other truths nowadays, felt but relative; the mails still bring rejection, though less.

In 1963, Judy Burroughs and I were married, and we moved—she from a tiny town called Landisville, in Pennsylvania, where she taught, and I a few blocks from Charles Street in the Village—to 44A Morton Street. You walked through a wrought-iron gate between brownstones on one of the Village's serenest leafy streets, near the Hudson, and you passed a small garden and walked over flagstones to the first of two three-story wooden houses said to have been home to Aaron Burr's domestic staff.

We lived in the first house, on the ground floor. We could look through two windows onto the flagstone yard. Upstairs lived men who made a lot of noise and changed lovers with accompanying arguments and alarming information. One Sunday morning, sleeping in, the former Judy Burroughs of Pennsylvania and the former Freddy Busch of Brooklyn were wakened by a long, loud discussion in which the elements of lovemaking were minutely sketched by someone whose good friend was taxing his physiology. Grist for the mill, I thought. Judy, lighting a cigarette to simulate poise, set her hair on fire. Grist for the mill, I thought, after we beat the blue flames down.

Judy commuted to a Westchester school district from the Village, after some months, while I did very little besides look for work, find bad jobs, and quit them. But from November 1963 through February 1964, we were office help in a market-research firm. We, and a large number of out-of-work actors and writers, compiled data from forms filled out by users of experimental soapsuds. (People actually wrote that the product in question "made my wash come whiter, brighter," mimicking a TV ad of the day.) Grist for the mill, I thought as we labored long and singly. We had to pretend to be unmarried, since market-research firms thought couples an employment risk (fire one and the other would go sour on you). We cherished the fact of our marriage. It felt, on some winter nights, like a crucial secret we carried back into the darkness of Morton Street. We were ratified in marriage because we hid the name of marriage from the philistines—who, not incidentally, did much to keep us fed.

We had seven dollars each week for food. Our rent was eighty-four dollars per month. Judy had four hundred dollars from her Pennsylvania retirement fund, and we brought in enough (thanks to the philistines) to keep us going. For our first Christmas, we gave each other a single paperback copy of *The Family of Man.* I don't apologize for our sentimentality: We loved each other taxingly, hopefully, stupidly, and dearly. We had no money for a Christmas tree because in the city anything that's vegetable and not dead costs more than a human life. I had stashed three dollars away, though, and at 11:45 on Christmas Eve of 1963, I stole out to Seventh Avenue, where a man who sold trees for far too much sold me the runt of his litter (it came, at most, to my waist). Judy cut paper chains for it and I spent until 2:00 A.M. trying to fashion a stand from wood given and tools lent by Marie Alexander, who was janitor for our buildings and an accomplished painter with oil on canvas. I failed to build the stand, as I have failed to build nearly everything from 1963 to the present, so I strung wire and cord from each corner of the room, and I suspended the tree, using a bumbled bowline around its tip, in the center of my inept web. It was an artifice built of failure and affection, the best I could do. The tree floated and swayed, and the paper chains rustled, and Judy laughed, and it was a most excellent Christmas because we were what we had dreamed to be—in love, and undefeated in New York.

The room in which the tree swayed was the whole apartment. It was about sixteen feet squared. My boyhood bookshelves were our cupboards and counter. An industrial sink was nearby, in the same corner of the room as our thigh-high refrigerator, attached to which was a waist-high stove with four gas burners, above which was attached our head-high oven. All were near the large stone fireplace, and to waken Judy on winter mornings, since our small radiators rarely offered heat enough to stir the icy air, I had to turn the oven on and open its door after building a fire in the fireplace with scrap wood found by Marie.

Crammed into our room was an armchair from Judy's apartment, and a table from her parents' dining room, and too many wooden chairs, and, of course, our double bed. I kept it covered with a red plaid blanket, for I was embarrassed lest strangers intuit its possible functions. Off our room was a bathroom, all ours, and very large. And there, at night, after our days of market research or job hunting, or rage—as on the day we quit a clerical job because the uptown vendor charged us ten cents for a candy bar, instead of the universal nickel—there is where I wrote.

I had a portable typewriter, given me by my parents when I left for college. I sat on the edge of our enormous bathtub, rested the typewriter on top of the closed toilet, and, while Judy slept, I wrote. In those days, I needed little sleep—I was twenty-two—and I was going to be a writer, I *was* a writer, I was going to get *them* to admit that I was a writer, and I sat in that awkward position and wrote my awkward prose. I was a failed poet. In graduate school, I'd admitted that I did not know where the poetic lines ought to end; I'd stopped ending them, had run them over from a justified margin, and had made prose narratives out of my terrible poems. But I still loved the music of poetry, and I tried still for poetry's concision, and its possibilities for a young man to sound like some Dylan Thomas of the short story. I larruped and looped, wove and wobbled, sank and rose and drifted on the languor of my lines. I was a very bad prose writer, and among the editors of magazines (and, later, books) in New York City, I was nicknamed "Promising," and was rejected all the time.

I wrote more, because I knew that I was bright—my parents and my college professors had told me so—and because I knew that it was only a matter of time and mere fortune before I arrived. I wrote a story called "Myself, a Yielder," about a girl I had loved in Brooklyn in the late fifties. I couldn't know that I would not get it right until 1979, after it had grown from nine typed pages to forty, and had still been rejected by a dozen magazines. I wrote a story called "Alma Mater," subtitled "The

Story of a Grocer." Always out of work, I wrote a story called "A Job of Work." I wrote a story called "Going to Christmas." It was about my mother, and it contained all the love and heartbreak you'd expect of my mother's brilliant baby boy traveling with trepidation into adulthood. Judy, wonderful friend, permitted me to send twenty-five dollars—how had she helped us to scrape it up? where, in those days, did such sums come from?—to the Scott Meredith Agency. Nobody then knew to advise me not to pay for a reading, so I sent my twenty-page story off, and, signed by Mr. Meredith himself, it said, a two-page letter came back.

It said that only if his agency helped and encouraged new writers could it "retain its place as a vital and thriving force in the community of letters." I was nearly in the community of letters! "You qualify," the letter told me, as a talented writer! "Your characterizations are excellent; your descriptive passages are evocative; your dialogue moves smoothly along. . . . These virtues are commendable, and I think you've got a lot of potential." And then the shoe, for which I'd been waiting, fell: Plotting, it seemed, was my "bête noire." Mr. Meredith addressed himself to plotting in general for some paragraphs before going on to tell me that my story, in particular, was awful, so bad, he said, that "I can't suggest a rewrite." So there I was. Call me "Promising."

Judy told me to chuck the letter, suggesting that the letter was a formula meant to entice me to send another story and another twenty-five dollars. But what writer chucks *any* letter in which his name is spelled correctly, in which he is recognized as having a lot of potential, and in which it says that all he has to do is conquer the black beast of awful and unrevisably inferior plotting? I put the letter in my "Market Information" folder and Judy hugged me hard, as if to make up for what I now think must have been resonances of doubt she felt in response to Mr. Meredith's letter. But she didn't let on. She was, after all, the same dear person who had sat in my apartment for hours as I wooed her by reading her every story I had written. So I didn't surrender. I wrote more stories—"Doris Day Loves Darwin," one was called, in which I mastered the art of imitating the prose rhythms of Bernard Malamud while showing none of his talent. I used an Irish name so that no one would suspect I was copying him.

Shortly thereafter, I rediscovered Faulkner and went on to imitate him. My first long work was a novella (really a novel gone dead) called *There Is No Phenix*. It might have been subtitled *A Kid from Brooklyn Rewrites As I Lay Dying*. But I wrote. Nearly every night, and often on Sunday afternoons—Saturdays were for Judy and me to sleep and to walk in the city—I did write. And a friend *did* point to a man, sitting with his back to us, reading a newspaper, in a coffeehouse called the Limelight—this was before it served liquor, when you could make a twenty-cent coffee last for all of that week's *Village Voice*—and say, "That's Thomas Pynchon." And I did not know who he was, nor did I care. I wanted people to be pointing to *my* back, saying *my* name. When asked, of course, I made it clear that my only interest in writing was the "service of art."

We moved to Bedford Street, also in the Village—three rooms! a shower! a kitchenette!—and Judy started teaching in Westchester, while I began the first of several nasty writing jobs. For a while, I helped my first "publishing" employer—he and I were the firm—to plagiarize government documents, available free, into simpler English that might be useful to the Hispanic-American constituency my boss hoped to serve. I quit after two weeks. There were other jobs, and we had a more lavish Christmas in 1964, and then we moved out to Harrison, New York, where we lived without a car and, literally, on the wrong side of the New York Central tracks. Judy was closer to her work, and I to mine (by then, I worked for a magazine in nearby Greenwich, Connecticut), and I wrote my first novel.

It was called *Coldly by the Hand*. I wrote it at night, after writing magazine talk all day, and my brain was always mushy and words no longer sounded true—they were notes heard from too great a distance. But I wrote it every night, and I finished it, and I typed it all over and then sent it off. And when Judy had helped me to discover that I despised the work I did and that I wanted to return to someplace I thought safer for one's sense of language and for work that didn't make me feel ashamed, we moved from Harrison to Hamilton, New York, a couple of hundred miles up and toward the center of the state. And in my first week as teacher of freshman composition at Colgate—six thousand dollars per year, and all the weekly themes I could eat—I had a letter from Atlantic Monthly Press.

The immensely kind, decent, encouraging and gentle Esther Yntema of that house broke the news to me that my novel had been rejected. She had encouraged me for nearly six months, and that sort of encouragement is underrated, usually by the writers who have received it, but it is stupendously important, and it still is given freely, and it goes far. You lie in bed at night, or walk across a windy campus, or lick at glue in an office with brown air, and you hear the phrase "enormous talent," written by one who ought to know, and you are like a patient receiving plasma who feels the needle slide in: You know it's not all over, you know it is one day going to be wonderful, and you know that someone's caring for you—you are *not*, in a cruel profession, alone. I sent the rejected novel to other publishers and wrote two more books.

I would like to report this now, because every writer dreams of it, and perhaps a new writer will read this and know that it actually can happen. I had sent my third novel (the other two never have been, never will be, published) to a friend then living in Scotland. He is Robert Nye, a fine poet, novelist, and critic now living in Ireland. His letters nourished me in 1965, when I started *Coldly* (the title is from a poem he wrote), and on through 1970, when I sent him my third novel, called *I Wanted a Year Without Fall.* Judy and I had returned from a trip to New York in February 1970. A friend had been at our house to care for our dog. She left us a note: One of us was to call Western Union. We did, and here's the message Western Union passed along: CALDER ACCEPTS YOUR NOVEL. CONGRATULATIONS. It was from Robert. It seems that he liked the novel and showed it to his publishers, Calder and Boyars, in London. Marion Boyars liked the novel enough to offer two hundred pounds. In those days, that amounted to $478. It took Mrs. Boyars from February until June to pay me for world rights to my book. I knew at the time that I was giving too much and getting too little, but I had no agent to lean on, and I had no strength for much resistance or negotiation—*it* was beginning, and I didn't want to do anything to jeopardize *it.* And though I was not to be published in the United States, by blessed New Directions and more blessed James Laughlin, until 1974, *it* had indeed begun. *It* didn't feel like an orchestra-backed moment in the movies, and there was surely no instant wealth, and, surely, there was less fame. But I was being published—after seven years of sending manuscripts out, I was going to see a book of mine published—and Judy and I sat down in our shabby living room in our rented house and we got drunk, and more on the intoxicating release of pressure from those years of waiting than on the bite and burn of the cheap whiskey we barely were able to afford and which we hardly remembered to swallow.

Two documents signify my young writer's life. The worst comes first. I read and reread it, in the early sixties and the late sixties and the early seventies, because it told me there was possibility even in what felt like wholesale failure. Harold Matson, who was Malcolm Lowry's agent—a generous one—sent it to him in 1941, saying, "I have regretfully come to the conclusion that I am not going to find a publisher for *Under the Volcano.*" The text of which I speak is the list that accompanied that note:

Farrar & Rinehart
Harcourt, Brace
Houghton Mifflin
Alfred Knopf
J. B. Lippincott
Little, Brown
Random House
Scribner's
Simon & Schuster
Duell, Sloan & Pearce
Dial Press
Story Press

These publishers declined an early version of that great novel. This list of them is owned by every writer I know, in his or her own analogous edition. For *Coldly by the Hand,* in a penmanship that looks familiar yet strangely young to me, inscribed in 1966 and 1967, I find this list:

Atlantic–Little, Brown	NO
Seymour Lawrence Assoc.	NO
David McKay Co.	NO
Atheneum	NO
Viking	NO
Putnam's	NO
Houghton Mifflin	NO
Scribner's	NO
Farrar, Straus & Giroux	NO

I acknowledged that my novel about two college professors I adored, and two young women I lusted after, was not quite *Under the Volcano.* But those parallel lists meant that we, Lowry and I, were brother sufferers and therefore brother writers. For we both, then, knew or had known the long pause, like the breath you take before ducking your head underwater, and then its terrible extension, like keeping your head underwater, and then its nasty conclusion, like being forced as you gasp for breath to go back under the water before you're ready. That was how it felt, sending the manuscript off, with its awful letter of clever chat. And then there was the waiting and speculating and fantasizing about the book's acceptance, the book's *adoration*, and then getting back the usually polite and often graceful but always unambiguous *No*. Lowry's pain was curiously sustaining, then, and I returned to it for company. And perhaps it is worth adding, for those who do not believe in hope and perseverance and the need to *erode* resistance by raining one's work steadily upon the editorial soil, that the first firm on Lowry's list and the last firm on mine finally did publish novels by me in 1980 and in 1981: dreams can (almost) come true.

The other text is dated three years earlier than my list—*Esquire* for July 1963. It was their issue on writers and writing, and the best I've seen since I started to read the magazine. That was the issue that helped me to define the context of what I was beginning to see as a career. Gay Talese wrote of the expatriates of the fifties who fled to Paris "In Search of Hemingway." In those days, most young writers still were in search of Hemingway's genius, and some—I am among them—consider at least one of his novels and many of his stories to be as good as anything American fiction offers. So not only was I sniffing at the stoop of *Paris Review* and the Deux Magots, I was inhaling some second- or thirdhand Hemingway; he taught us that the artist was a soldier on the page, a priest who had sex: We might dismiss the heady mix as youth, but we could not dismiss its seductiveness. Norman Mailer, Hemingway's Oedipal son in those days—art was the mother and wife—reviewed recent work by his colleagues, saying honestly how he saw them as adversaries in his sweepstakes, and telling some fascinating truth about some misunderstood writers; his comments on

James Jones's *The Thin Red Line*, and on postwar writing in general, still hold up. There were excerpts of works in progress (some of which still haven't seen light), and I felt, as I looked through the issue again and again, that I lived near the house of fiction, that I soon must find a way in.

Theodore and Renee Weiss gave me my first American publication in their *Quarterly Review of Literature* (in 1966); Wayne Carver was hospitable at *Carleton Miscellany;* and Ted Solotaroff, launching *New American Review*, was warm and encouraging—he was the first editor to solicit my work and then to take some and then to pay a decent wage. And while there continued to be cruelty afoot, and stupidity, and editorial laziness; while editors couldn't read and wouldn't read a manuscript—unless it was by Richard Brautigan or the author of *Love's Flaring Nostrils:* Those were the literary poles; while an agent did write to say that he liked my letter of inquiry more than the prose of my fiction—there nevertheless *was* scrupulous reading being given to serious writing, mine generously included. And editorial taste, for which there is precious little accounting, was, in fact, exercised with some conscience.

During the early days of *New American Review*, for example, its editor, Ted Solotaroff, received a story by Robert Stone. The story sent to Solotaroff is brilliant, it sums up a good deal of the sixties and of American romanticism, and it is a marvelous transmogrification: Read an account of the actual incident in Tom Wolfe's *The Electric Kool-Aid Acid Test*, and then see how Stone makes art out of madness in his "Porque No Tiene, Porque Le Falta," which is reprinted in Stone's *Bear and His Daughter.*

Despite its quality, *NAR* was not always the first choice of many agents and authors. For during those days of the late sixties and early seventies, *Harper's* was publishing risky fiction and was paying well for it; *Esquire* was becoming a showcase for new writing; *The New Yorker* was stirred by some life. These were the places fiction went first, and then to *NAR*, and then to the smaller literary quarterlies (they could offer at most a readership of a few thousand, and not much payment).

So Stone's long story might well have had its last chance for reasonably wide readership and decent pay for its author when it was returned from *NAR*. Solotaroff rejected it. As he told me, he declined the story because it seemed excessively romantic. On the other hand, he said, he could not forget parts of it. An experienced editor, he listened to his inner voice and he sent for the story, then published it. This example of taste accounting for itself, and of grace notes sung louder than the music of woe, was sustaining at the time and remains so today.

Aspects of the taste for which there's—usually—no accounting became known to me in forceful personal terms when, in 1972, I wrote a short story called "Widow Water." I sent it to *NAR* and Ted Solotaroff sent it back. *Harper's* declined it next. Then Gordon Lish, the fiction editor at *Esquire*, rejected it. At this point, an agent took charge of my professional life and the story was sent to, and was sent back by, fiction editors at six other magazines.

In 1973, it went to *Paris Review* and George Plimpton accepted "Widow Water" and published it in 1974. In December of 1974, my agent received a letter from Gordon Lish, asking why he hadn't ever seen the story and saying he wished that he'd been given a chance to publish it. When told that he'd declined it two years before, he was amazed.

The story was reprinted in an anthology published in 1977, a time when I was finishing a novel and starting to assemble a volume of short stories. Like many writers who went from poems to stories to novels, I believe in economy—deleted lines and paragraphs in fiction, even deleted stories from collections. So I didn't include "Widow Water" in the original short-story manuscript I put together for my editor at Harper & Row (now HarperCollins). The collection was declined—"A collection of short fiction is not advisable for you at this stage of your career,"

I was told—and I went back to my Lowry list, not touched by such solicitude, and aware that story collections were actually, at times, scary to book editors. But I was luckier than many. My book of stories *Hardwater Country* was accepted by another house within two weeks. My new editor? The former fiction editor at *Esquire*, who had already published two stories of mine.

Lish and I prepared *Hardwater Country* for publication, and we decided that I'd cut too many stories. I took six or seven with me to New York, and Lish, after some hard reading, concluded that a story new to him, "Widow Water," should be added to the book. Lish read that story superbly, he edited it brilliantly, and I honestly believe that he understood it better than I did. But it was brand-new to him. And when I told him he'd seen it, he insisted that I was wrong. I didn't argue. It's nearly impossible to persuade an editor to convince his or her seniors to bring a book of stories out. This bright man was *volunteering*. I was grateful, despite the low advance and lack of any advertising.

Hardwater Country was published. A reviewer for the daily *New York Times* savaged it, complaining of "modern fiction" in general and my brand of it in particular. He made it clear that the talkative and emotional plumber who narrates "Widow Water" was for him an example of "modern fiction" at its worst. Months later, when the book had already been returned to the warehouse, a reviewer in the *New York Times Book Review* wrote that "the best piece in this admirable collection is . . . a monologue by a plumber who performs his trade with the skill and sensitivity of an old-fashioned country doctor." Again, I was grateful, confused, and, of course, disappointed; my "doctor" apparently would live, but my book had died. And then there is this: In the *New York Times*, the same daily reviewer, writing on his life in Connecticut some time after the publication of my book, wrote at length about his talkative plumber. A friend sent me the column, attached to a note that said, "Aren't you glad his pump got primed?" No, I wasn't, I have to confess. I still hated

the feeling generated by serving as the source of a cruel reviewer's comment on my own book (in small part) and a fuller
exposition on the subject—usually him- or herself—that was of
more interest to the writer holding forth in that day's paper. As
my plumber might have said, the water that primes a pump is
swallowed down, then swilled around in the pump's mechani-
cal innards. As the pump begins to draw, the priming water is
spewed up and out. A book that took years to make—never
mind with what difficulties—becomes a mouthful of metal-
colored spit.

One reason for telling this story is that in this profession
there is little logic. Editors, dealing with art so very personally
made, make personal decisions. There so rarely is or can be
any accounting for their taste. To be sure, editors are fired, and
for a variety of reasons. They are usually not fired, though, for
letting interesting works of fiction that won't sell tens of thousands of copies slide from the slippery desk and back to their authors. Their life isn't easy, and despite jokes about editorial
lunches, and despite one's disagreements with many editors'
taste, there is good reason to remember fondly, say, Ted
Solotaroff and Esther Yntema.

IT CAME PRETTY TRUE. We live in a farmhouse on a wild
ridge above Sherburne, New York. Some of my neighbors know
that I write things, and they don't hold it against me. Most of
them don't know. From the back of our house, you can look
over long fields to the town of Edmeston, and even toward
Cooperstown. It is some of the handsomest rough country I
know. On wonderful days, I think more about the land, about
our two sons, even about our awful cats and fine dogs, and, of
course, about Judy than I do about matters I call "professional"—the placing of my work in magazines and between
hard covers and soft, and the terrible task of trying to manage

whatever talent I was born with and energy I haven't squandered.

When I'm writing a book or story, I think about that work in progress all the time. And then I rarely, except when not sitting at the keyboard, think about the "professional" part. I call it that because what I do when I write is amateur—I do it for love, because of compulsive need, out of a requirement that I cannot shake: that I justify my time on the earth by telling stories. That's what I do. I have to do it.

But the "professional" part—the stuff people ask about after readings, the ugly information writers trade at awkward parties—I do because I love my amateur work and love some of what I've written and like a lot of it and even respect a quantity of it; it would be dishonorable to try less than my best on its behalf. (Before you snort with derision: Of *course* I would like to be rich; of *course* I would like to be the Gary Cooper of American letters.)

Indeed, I think that I do not think at all when I write. As I used to sit at my battered, topless, sticky, and chipped Royal 440 manual, I now sit at the keyboard of my old-fashioned DOS-driven word processor, and—it remains my verb of choice—I type. He says, and then she says, and then they see something or hear it or learn it somehow, and then someone else makes her say to him what, it occurs to me as the story begins to close its arc and end, the story seems to have been wanting to be about. I think of myself as a jock, a verbal athlete. I move on the page in certain ways because long practice has taught me how to move best, and long needing has made me try to do it better, in new ways pleasing to my secret longings and the readers I want very much to reach and please.

I've written about children modeled after my children and about parents modeled after my parents. I have written about women I loved when young and—best, when I've really been cooking at the keyboard—about women I would love to love whether old, young, or, as I like to think of myself now, as somewhat squarely in the middle. My friend Elaine Markson, who is my agent, says that no matter how imagined I say my female characters are, my female protagonists are modeled, one way or another, near or far, after the former Judy Burroughs.

In *Rounds*, published in 1979, there's a woman named Lizzie Bean, who is, I feel, cast away by my male protagonist, a doctor named Eli Silver. When I regretted to a friend that I had served Lizzie Bean poorly, my friend said, "All women get cast away, Fred. That's why they keep ending up in novels." But I wasn't reassured. Because I modeled her physically and probably psychically after Judy, my wife, I wanted to do better by Ms. Bean. I had to rescue her.

In my 1986 novel, *Sometimes I Live in the Country*, I plucked Lizzie Bean from the frozen-fowl section of the Price Chopper supermarket in Bennington, Vermont, and I tried to transport her to the sort of life she deserved. And of course it had to do, that life, with being at a farmhouse on a wild ridge in the hills above a place like Sherburne, New York. And Lizzie deserved a decent man with whom she could share what time she wished to share. I didn't, therefore, give her a writer to love.

But neither could I leave her alone. I had a very difficult time beginning a novel published in 1993, *Long Way from Home*. I didn't feel comfortable with the woman who would be at its core until I realized that Lizzie Bean, now a rural public-school principal and the wife of a small-town newspaper editor, was the hero of my story. Her husband isn't much of an editor or writer, and that's why she is able to love him, I think. Lizzie would have been displeased to live with a man who so wants attention, approval, a readership whose emotion is a kind of love. For many writers, after awhile, the only way the world, using its hard language, can assure them of its love is by giving the writers money. It is what the world most begrudges the writer and what its gossip columns discuss most in the writer's life. When he receives currency, he knows that he is the possessor of the cruel world's heart.

Charles Dickens, one of the most energetic world-wooers, wrote about *Nicholas Nickleby*, first published in monthly installments: "the Author of these pages, now lays them before his readers in a completed form, flattering himself . . . that on the first of next month they may miss his company at the accustomed time as something which used to be expected with pleasure. . . ." In his preface to *David Copperfield*, he addresses "the reader whom I love." Dickens could never let his readers go; he always spoke to them, in his prefaces, because he left their company with such reluctance. He so wanted to be loved by his readers that he went out to meet them, giving dozens upon dozen of readings, in England and the United States, until he died as the result of an overexertion that was, I think, worthwhile to him. For he could stand before his readers and know, from their applause and their tears and their fainting into the aisles, that they loved him. Would Lizzie Bean's husband be different, except in degree, if he were a writer? I doubt it. How difficult it might be for Lizzie, then, to live with a man who, no matter how well he tried to love her, might be trying at least equally hard to woo a world of strangers.

And there is this reason, again exemplified by Dickens, this time on his completion of *The Old Curiosity Shop*: ". . . writing until four o'Clock this morning, finished the old story [in which Little Nell dies]. It makes me very melancholy to think that all these people are lost to me for ever, and I feel as if I never could become attached to any new set of characters." It couldn't lessen difficulties for Lizzie if she knew that Dickens deeply mourned the passing of each set of characters: He expresses the "reluctance and regret" he feels in leaving "my visionary friends" from *Martin Chuzzlewit;* he sorrows painfully over Paul Dombey's death in *Dombey and Son;* the man whose wife—he threw her out, Lizzie, for a younger woman, an actress!—bore them ten children refers to *David Copperfield* as his "favourite child." Lizzie would be living with a man who passionately loved his characters and those strangers he required for audience. That is a good deal of competition, even for a woman as strong and attractive as Lizzie. (She is *so* strong, you may have noted, that I am writing about her as if she is true. If circumstances may be tough for Lizzie Bean, how easy can they be for Judy Busch?)

And then there is this for Lizzie to consider: So many writers are self-lovers even more than they are lovers of their characters or readers. In the making of art, after all, lie so many possibilities for the making of love to oneself; writing can be a frictive as well as a fictive experience. One is listening to oneself because one is doomed to, from birth, if a writer; the process of surviving in that profession, with such a curse of inwardness *and* outwardness, is one of learning that a seamless fusion of inner and outer worlds produces art; the rest is either masturbation, if too much inner world dominates, or good journalism, if the outer world holds sway. The danger is that one must invite as much as possible of each world into the mind and onto the page (at least in early drafts). But all too frequently, the writer can forget to listen to everything except the self—it speaks so sexily. Writing, then, is a test of character; the ones who pass are merely doing what their trade requires, while the ones who fail are doing what comes, alas, quite naturally. An acquaintance of mine, a writer whose work is published often enough, assures us, in a published interview, of "the world of emotional extremity" in which he lives, adding rather exquisitely that, while "all people walk over it," only he and his fellows-of-sensibility "are doomed to live there." He says that "the pain, frustration and torment of this calling takes its toll." Imagine, then, that Lizzie Bean comes home from a tough day at school. She and her husband pour out drinks, sit in the living room, and begin to trade stories in the ordinary domestic debriefing that goes on between mates. Lover boy suddenly wags his pipe at her and impatiently shakes his head, requesting silence: She may have "walked over" the terrain of emotional extremity, he tells his beloved, but *he has been living there*, don't forget, just on the other side of the psychic tollbooth.

No. I'm too much of a realist to want to write a potential self-lover into the life of a woman who needs some company. I'm too much of a lover of my own characters to want Lizzie Bean living with a man who might love his characters or his public or the nauseous sentimental self more than he loves her. I'll not let her love a writer.

And, while I've dared to imitate aspects of my wife in order to make a Lizzie Bean whom I can love, though she mustn't love the likes of me, I have worked at *not* writing fiction about the first Christmas together of me and the former Judy Burroughs. I think that I am waiting for the right—the perfect—fiction for that image, a context in which that wonderful ugly tree, tied, in the air, to the corners of our first apartment, can be useful in a grand story while remaining completely the runt Christmas tree of 1963. Fiction writers are sworn by the nature of their work to such fealties. They deal with matters of the earth, with objects of specific gravity. I believe that I and my brothers and sisters in writing strive to keep our feet as firmly on the ground as Judy's Christmas tree and mine was off it. I believe that we remain writers because we return to that striving each time—as here, now—we fail.

Part Two

"*You know I like you less and less the more I know you.*"
"*Madame, it is always a mistake to know an author.*"

—Ernest Hemingway, *Death in the Afternoon*

BAD

In the practice of my trade, as writer and teacher, I lie by omission, I sometimes think, as much as I tell the truth. I note, for an eager, untalented first-year student, that her story is *interesting*, that it *shows terrific energy*, that *there's some marvelous insight here* into waking up hungover on Saturday morning after a debauched night at ATO. At summer writers' conferences, I am not about to tell a seventy-year-old woman that her personal diaries, recorded since World War II and bound in leather, need to be buried or burned before she can think to write what consumes her, the story of her life. In book reviews, it is unusual when you or I say, outright, that a book by one of our colleagues is ordinarily lousy.

Mercy is all to the good, and maybe it's another name for being afraid—often for obvious, sometimes honorable, reasons—of telling what seems to be the truth. But sometimes I find myself, as I read a set of essays for school, or put down a stranger's galleys after not many pages, wanting to stand, and flap my featherless wings, and howl that, goddamn it, this is outright bad. I've been thinking about what constitutes badness, and reflecting on the pleasures of announcing its presence in the room.

Bad, I recall, was once good. In novels and poems—and especially at poetry readings—of the fifties and early sixties, to call a musician or writer bad was to say he was excellent beyond words. Because jazz was the music of the revolution, and because the best musicians were black or admirably, like Gerry Mulligan, blackened in their art, the sense of life as protest, the sighing song about being Beat, was punctuated by what used to be called "negritude." When one was good at being in a state of protest, at being, through one's art, not only accomplished (conventionally good) but also avant-garde and crazy with this life and showing it, one was bad (*un*conventionally good). Norman Mailer wanted the badness of *The White Negro* but wasn't, he might in his seventies admit of himself in the sixties, good enough.

Nowadays, if you're bad, you no longer swing: You dance to rap; you fight the power by wearing angry T-shirts and by doing what, if you're white, you think black people do. If you're black and smart, like Stanley Crouch or Ernest J. Gaines or Toni Morrison or David Bradley, you've been watching the white folk strive to be bad while you've labored to make your work as good as you can.

Bad, in other words, is protest and Perrier unless the badness takes place in the real arenas of race—the streets or the voting booth or sometimes the page. People who call themselves or others "bad," in that old-fashioned sense, are no longer good enough to get away with it.

Of course, conventional bad remains to us. Richard Nixon did well by doing bad. He was bad, he is bad, he died bad, and we will miss him because his badness helped to define what many of us think is, in public life, good. Vietnam was bad. The invasion of Grenada was bad. The failure of nerve by the West in Bosnia was bad. Desert Storm was done well for bad reasons; to the 100,000 non-Westerners who died in it, badness abounded. Our confrontation of Haiti began and will end badly. Hollywood's renditions of teachers and writers, no matter how many times they are attempted, are bad. Journeyman baseball players who earn a million dollars a year to hit .243 and play average infield represent something bad. Pop Warner football, with its emphasis on winning at every conceivable cost, before rapaciously howling parents, is bad. Spectators at Little League games tend to the bad. Television commercials for beer are bad. Songs on jukeboxes that take as their subject sundown, long nights, or truck rides are bad. Women who feel constrained to dress for business by looking like men and carrying cordovan attaché cases have been subjected to what's bad. MTV is bad. Press secretaries are bad. Plastic bottles for whiskey are bad. So is most Beaujolais nouveau and the fashion for giving it as a gift. So is the airplane announcement about "smoking materials." So is the seating space on the plane. The old *New Yorker* was bad. The Anglophile new *New Yorker* is bad. People who talk about the old or new *New Yorker* are bad. So are writers who comment on them. Men's vertically moussed haircuts are bad.

Bad is what you call an applicant for a job at a university who describes her method of teaching the writing of fiction "an empowerment of the gender-oppressed and racial minorities." She adds, promptly, that she has also found her method to work in "bringing out silenced white males." Which leaves us with no one to do the *oppression*, she forgot to say. She will be hired, I've no doubt, and will go on, canons firing, to become a star in some department. She will teach her students that they're victims. She will teach them how to prove it.

Also bad are literature professors who think that contemporary writing is, at its best, the cream in the departmental coffee. They tolerate writers, although it is their secret, they think, that Geoffrey Chaucer, were he to make application for work, would not be hired because he is a dead white European male and because his degree isn't good enough, and because he doesn't *do* theory. These people do not understand that literary art is not only the cream in their coffee but also the hillside on which the coffee is planted, the earth in which it is grown, the sweat on the skin of the men and women who pick the beans, the water in which the ground beans steep, the mouth that, savoring it, speaks by expelling words in shapes of breath it scents.

It is bad that black writers do being black, white writers only being white, Chicanos being Hispanic, lesbians being homosexual, and feminists being feminist—instead of each doing art, or professing English, or writing about the nature of the world that has the temerity to exist outside them. It is bad for their souls and our minds that careerism so drives their critical faculties and their prose. A young artist or professor knows that you achieve success now by writing, painting, composing, or critiquing by way of your genes and the color of your skin. Authors once strove to get good by being more than the total of their birth weight multiplied by their genetic code. It's bad that they now claim credibility (and royalty checks) on the basis of the accident of their birth.

In a burst of badness, Peter Brooks, in a review in the *Times Literary Supplement*, yawns that "We have known for some time that fictional characters are linguistic constructs, that the impression of mimesis of real persons that they may give is a mirage, and that to ask how many children Lady Macbeth had is the wrong way to interrogate literature." Professor Brooks bends backward into the professorial critical wars to recall the feud between A. C. Bradley and L. C. Knights, whose *How Many Children Had Lady Macbeth?* is evoked by his question. Brooks reminds us that Shakespeare's characters aren't, you know, real; they're, you know, language; when you speculate about the biology of a linguistic construct, you're believing in the language instead of prodding at it, disproving it. You aren't cool.

I am of the body-heat school, the school uncool. I think that to ask ourselves—so long as we don't require a specific number in reply—how many children Lady Macbeth might have had is to believe in her as a person on the page, a figure on the stage, and is to ask questions in *a* right way. Has she not sexed her husband past all inner and social restraint—meager as they might have been—and into dark, maddened criminality? What was she like in bed? we well might wonder. Was she cold and withholding? All nakedness and surrender? Did she claw at his flesh? Startle him with his own appetites? Do we not imagine about what's not made explicit? Is that not one reason for a writer to withhold instead of delineate? Does the writer not, him- or herself, speculate or intuit or *feel*—there, I've said the *F* word— about the secrets of his or her self as well as these metaphors for self, these people, pulled up from the page?

And note: Such thinking "is the wrong way to interrogate literature." Literature, then, is not studied or read; it is not considered or enjoyed: It is interrogated. Tie it in a chair beneath hot lights. Pump it full of chemicals. Apply electrodes to its most delicate parts. Beat it; steal its family; *disappear* it. The aggression in the word is noteworthy, and it is bloated with self-delight, with arrogance. We know the right way, that sure locution says. And it is bad, and a symptom of bad education in the graduate schools, and a guarantee of bad education by graduate students turned college professor and high school teacher, and an assurance, for years to come, of literary papers and essays and books that hum with contentment and cover the field—a living blanket of flies on the body of literature.

Mr. Brooks reminds us that "we really haven't found a vocabulary, or a conceptual framework, that takes us much beyond the formative cultural work done by Dickens, Tolstoy, George Eliot and the rest." Don't you love that "the rest"? Thackeray and Emily Brontë, Gaskell and Chekhov: the rest.

Why not think a moment of those Victorians, of those "the rest": Thomas Hardy, for example, clumsy and obsessed and brilliant in spite of a self-professed disdain for his own prose. He writes *Tess of the d'Urbervilles*, in 1891, intending, according to his subtitle, *A Pure Woman*, to assert that purity has less to do with having borne an illegitimate child and having committed adultery and having murdered the child's father and her adulterous partner than his readers might think.

Hardy presupposes Tess. He doesn't only write her: he believes in her. He doesn't see her as "an illusory ideological formation, another product of Western logocentric metaphysics," which is how Brooks defines character. "The concept of character," Brooks goes on, "is the reification of a figure, in which the sign itself ('character' as an engraved mark) is substituted for what it signifies ('character' as the traits constituting selfhood)."

Hardy didn't know that. He wrote about a woman he conceived as flesh and blood in his imagination and whom he tried to make tangible and persuasive on the page. He believed in her enough, the dolt who was "one of the rest," so that in the posthumously published putative biography of Hardy by his wife, Florence—it was actually his own grindingly discreet autobiography—he twice describes women to whom he was attracted in these terms: One had "quite a 'Tess' mouth and eyes: with these two beauties she can afford to be indifferent about the remainder of her face"; of the other he says, "In appearance she is something like my idea of 'Tess,' though I did not know her when the novel was written." Thomas Hardy is in love— with, I guess, "an illusory ideological formation."

I think, sometimes, that many postmodern critics do not love anything except the control they exercise in alleging the artist's uncontrol. They are well-fed revolutionaries, bourgeoisie in guerilla costumes. Their field is power, and some of it resides in their knowing what they say and your not knowing what they say because they use bird whistles, eyebrow twitches, invisible-ink codes, furtive-fingered recognition gestures, and secret handshakes understood mostly by them. I'd like to call that smug codification bad.

But I know as well as you that what's bad is also found in language perpetrated by writers in the name of love and of loving their characters. I am thinking of a first novel I won't name. It's done; the author can't be helped with this one, and there's always hope that someone—editors have been paid, in the past, for such work, and some have even done it—will warn him or her about such writing. In that novel, the birth of a child is exhaustingly awaited and then the child dies. The mother is crushed, but she plods on through her life. At the end, at a reception, a handsome restaurant owner asks her to dance. She "folded herself into" his arms, and they "sailed across the room." Those terms are of course bad: They are constructed of received language, and they are not speaking to us; they show that the writer believes he or she *is*, but we know he or she cannot be. For how does the human body fold itself into someone else's embrace without breaking or at least bending very painfully? How does it sail across a room unless someone has pitched it? The character ceases to be particular when expressed in such language; she here becomes an echo of ten thousand writers and ten thousand characters who enjoyed being held by a man while dancing. Each time a writer fails to particularize such a moment, a character dies, and we are left with television: the general idea of, the electronic signal about, a woman who dances. It's the jokester's convention, and the master of ceremonies calls out, "Number Eleven," and everyone knows to laugh.

Suddenly this character knows—but only because the author has decided that the book is going to end here—that "she had survived, it was all that mattered, to survive and endure and let go." She knows that "the future belonged to her." The handsome man dips her and she laughs. "Looking at the ceiling, she thought she heard soft applause, the sound of baby hands clapping."

Those are the last words of the novel. They are bad. They are failed feeling—the failure of a writer to find the right words about emotion: sentimentality, that is to say, and the careless use of language as a rhetorical weapon—to, in this case, bludgeon the reader into acceding to the novelist's postulations about emotional life. We know that we long to speak to the dead and to be consoled by them. And good writers have made this common knowledge uncommon. Here, the author has made this impulse embarrassing and the protagonist infantile. By asking the reader to be infantile, too, the author invites the sort of antagonism we reserve for baby talk between lovers we're not. Bad.

Also bad: *The Bridges of Madison County*, a *New York Times* best-seller for, it seems, most of my adult life. This paragon of dead prose is about a Marlboro Man photographer and the woman whom he makes beautiful with his great art. It was at first reviewed almost nowhere. Word of mouth made it sell so many copies, its author installed an 800 telephone number on which his enchanted readers could leave messages about their powerful response. In turn, book-chat people have begun to write as if they take the book seriously. The earning of money unfailingly has this effect.

The woman made beautiful says, "If you took me in your arms and carried me to your truck and forced me to go with you, I wouldn't murmur a complaint. You could do the same thing just by talking to me. But I don't think you will. You're too sensitive, too aware of my feelings, for that. . . . My life . . . lacks romance, eroticism, dancing in the kitchen to candlelight, and the wonderful feel of a man who knows how to love a woman. . . ."

The next morning, as cowboys who know how to satisfy a woman always do after satisfying her, he leaves. "Her mind was gone, empty, turning. 'Don't leave, Robert Kincaid,' she could hear herself crying out from somewhere inside."

Why is this bad? The entire phenomenon is bad—the work itself, and its enormous popularity, which tells us that we, as a reading populace, are in love with what's bad. What we love, apparently, is talk that doesn't sound like people but that does sound like speeches made by a person on the page, written by someone who doesn't listen to the rest of the world or know how to make plausible an imitation of the world. If you agree with me, you are asking for homage to the world in what you read, not homage to theory about " 'character' as an engraved mark."

If you agree with me, you know that the dialogue I quoted from the novel is a summary of points—he's sensitive, she's needful, and he is a dervish in her cold bed—and not the statement of a soul with whom your soul, you feel, needs communion. Indeed, then, you probably believe in something like souls and something like communion which is available, without brain death, to readers.

If you agree with me, you marvel (to say the least) at a woman whose mind not only is "gone" but is in its absence still present enough to record that it is "empty" and that, while vanished and hollow, it is "turning." While turning stomachs are appropriate, perhaps, a turning mind suggests something like those whirling plastic barrels from which women in tights pluck lottery winners on cable TV. Note further, please, that while her mind is both gone *and* enough on the scene to record its empty *tour jeté*, it can assist her to "hear herself crying out from somewhere inside." You can only cry "out" from someplace that's in, of course; so logic is not what the statement's about, but emotion. She hears herself with a mind that's not there, yet, turning, cries out when she does not, in fact, cry out. It's a silent cry, then, and yet the author feels the need to tell us that it's "from somewhere inside." From where else?

This is the language of television, of bodice rippers, of the Harlequin Romance. It is incapable and irresponsible writing, unmediated by thought or the gift of artifice, or by the author's belief in a character sufficient to move him. It's what the majority of readers seem to want. That's bad.

What's good, then? Am I not defending the old-fashioned and ignoring the hard-edged new? Well, the hard-edged new is old, I'm saying. No one has yet written a more profoundly moving, vast, and encompassing novel in America than Melville did in his *Moby-Dick* of 1851. Surely it is the template by which we judge both our jokes about and our attempts to write—or, as readers, to find—the Great American Novel. William Gaddis's *The Recognitions*, Ralph Ellison's *Invisible Man*, Thomas Pynchon's *Gravity's Rainbow*, Eudora Welty's *Losing Battles*, Maureen Howard's *Natural History:* These come to mind as candidates; each is vast, encyclopedic, steeped in American history and in the lives of characters about whose fate we care. Only in the Pynchon are the characters flat, two-dimensional— commentary, in effect, on the difficulty of dealing in contemporary terms with emotion. The others, including the Melville, deal with *feeling* as well as intellection. Remember that *Moby-Dick* begins with an 1851 rendition of the blues ("Whenever I find myself growing grim about the mouth; whenever it is a damp, drizzly November in my soul; whenever I find myself involuntarily pausing before coffin warehouses, and bringing up the rear of every funeral I meet").

Contemporary fiction of the unemotional sort plays off the emotions it seems to forswear; the narrator—these are usually first-person novels—manifests the pain he or she then insists he or she doesn't care about and that the prose, it's insisted, doesn't reflect. And then the author factors the pain into his or her pas-

sages, so that you feel them on the author's behalf. At its clum-
siest, we have the author turning you into a parent or lover and
you're feeling just terrible on his or her behalf. At its best, we
have *L'Etranger* with a chaser. "Mother died," Meursault announces, and then he boasts that he can't recall when. We respond by supplying the emotion our protagonist claims not to
feel. Our participation in that transaction consists of this: We
have endured a parent's death, or we fear it, or fear our own,
and fear for the strength of our love, or fear to be *un*loved. We
are loyal to those tawdry elements of life, that is to say, that a
professional postmodernist pretends to believe one can afford
to put, as they like to term it, under erasure. But they are
human, and we are, too, and the fiction we read for our souls'
sake—and not for the sake of advancing our careers—is what
responds to our humanness. Find out which detective stories
about passion and trespass your neighborhood theorist reads
during the campus vacation.

If you don't agree with me, give up: You will. You will remember the death of a parent, the loss of a friend, the terror or
illness of a child you tried to protect. It is those moments—they
are lived at body temperature; there is nothing cool about
them—that define a life. In the art about which you're serious,
you seek, willy-nilly, examinations of and metaphors about the
heat of your existence. Even if your blood has run cold, you
don't want anybody else being cool about such times. They are
your times, and you were on the face of this earth and in trou-
ble or love, and while you are perfectly willing to be attrac-
tively disenchanted and invulnerable in public when you need
to, you know that the warmth of flesh, the muddiness of earth,
the terror of madness and death, the hugeness of institutions,
and the brevity of your life and the lives of those you need are
what your seriousness involves. Such moments help you to define your morality. You seek them and it in the art you make or
surrender to.

What resorts to trend and gossip, to evasion and gloss, to the cutely second-rate, or what drops its bucket all the little inches down into the muck and gravel of jargon and career, is the opposite of what your soul requires, and it's bad. And maybe what is worst is the noise of some tired writer who, preaching and confessing, flaps his unfeathered wings in your face. Doesn't he know better?

MELVILLE'S MAIL

WHEN HE WAS thirty-three, he felt finished. The book he knew to be special—it "is of the horrible texture of a fabric that should be woven of ships' cables & hausers," he wrote; "a Polar wind blows through it, & birds of prey hover over it"— had failed. American and English reviewers had roasted *Moby-Dick* (1851) and in eighteen months the American edition sold 2,300 copies. *Pierre* (1852) sold 2,030 copies over thirty-five years. It earned Melville the scorn of reviewers—they questioned his sanity as well as his skill—and, by the end of his life, a total of $157.

He had to worry about money, for he farmed a little, but he counted on the harvest of his writing, and his wife's small trust fund, for the support of their family. This support was threatened, and since money is a letter from the world to an author about his work, Melville had to face up to the prospect of not getting across his doubting dark vision; for he received too little of the mail that would have assured him that he was heard. As he had complained, in a letter to Hawthorne, in 1851: "Dollars damn me; and the malicious Devil is forever grinning in upon me, holding the door ajar. . . . I shall be worn out and perish, like an old nutmeg grater, grated to pieces by the constant attrition of the wood, that is, the nutmeg. What I feel most moved to write, that is banned—it will not pay. Yet, altogether, write the *other* way I cannot. So the product is a final hash, and all my books are botches."

The well-received author of travel and adventure stories such as *Typee* (1846) and *Mardi* (1849) had become the student of Shakespeare's and Carlyle's works, the hard questioner of heavenly works, and the man whose soul had resonated in response to the works of Nathaniel Hawthorne—"there is the blackness of darkness beyond," he wrote of Hawthorne's tales, and he praised "those short, quick probings at the very axis of reality" which had "dropped germinous seeds into my soul." Melville had lost what ease he'd possessed, and now his work would lose its. Into *Moby-Dick*, which he was writing as he wrote to Hawthorne, he put "the sane madness of vital truth," and the world didn't want to hear it.

And so we come to the exhausted Melville of 1852. He begins to speak—it is nearly impossible, still, for him to be silent—of what obsesses him: the failure of crucial messages to get through, and the condemnations to (or attractions of) silence. Such matters become central; they are the mail of which I speak.

It is likely that Melville had come to love Hawthorne: The handsome older writer, Melville wrote in "Hawthorne and His Mosses" in 1850, "shoots his strong . . . roots into the hot soil of my . . . soul." They were neighbors and saw each other, though less than Melville wished, and then Hawthorne moved away; they corresponded, exchanging books *(Pierre* for *The*

Blithedale Romance) and ideas. The case of Agatha Hatch Robertson was relayed by Melville. It involved a young wife who waited seventeen years for word—literally, for mail—from her husband, who had left to seek work. Melville here postulates to Hawthorne how the story of Agatha and her mailbox might be told: "As her hopes gradually decay in her, so does the post itself & the little box decay. The post rots in the ground *at last.* Owing to its being little used—hardly used at all—grass grows rankly about it. *At last* a little bird nests in it. *At last* the post falls." (My italics.)

It seems clear that this synopsis speaks for Melville. The story of abandonment and apprehensive waiting for messages is relevant to a writer in Melville's situation—he laments the undelivered incoming mail (the world's attention) and the outgoing mail (his writing) that does not get through. The nesting bird underscores not only the pathos of the disuse of the mailbox but also Melville's sense of his ridiculousness: Is he merely a white-stained post? And listen to the rhythm of the repetition of "at last" and "At last" and "At last": It is incantatory, funereal, and about Herman Melville's fatigue.

Melville had steeped himself in Shakespeare's tragedies as he prepared to write *Moby-Dick.* In "Mosses" he had said, "Through the mouths of the dark characters of Hamlet, Timon, Lear, and Iago, he [Shakespeare] craftily says, or sometimes insinuates, the things which we feel to be so terrifically true that it were all but madness for any good man, in his own proper character, to utter or even hint of them." Whenever he wrote of literature, Melville tended to write about the process of writing in general, and his own in particular; he does so above, homing in on his own relationship to Ahab, who—like Pierre—served as Melville's dark mask. Now he ventriloquized from within his notion of Agatha, and later he would use Claggert and Captain Vere.

It is Hamlet who speaks in the outline of the Agatha story.

Grass grows "rankly" around the rotting post; it is Hamlet who, lamenting religious injunctions against suicide, describing life as weary, stale, flat, and unprofitable, bemoaning the need for silence ("I must hold my tongue"), calls the world "an un-weeded garden" taken over by things "*rank* and gross" (my ital-ics). Melville was low enough in spirit to place himself in Hamlet's garden, and in Agatha's dooryard.

In October 1852, *Putnam's Magazine* invited him to con-tribute work. In December, he began to write the Agatha story. Unsurprisingly, he didn't complete it, for he had told its essen-tial elements to Hawthorne; and it was Agatha's situation, not self, that was dark and alive to Melville. She was his emblem more than his story. But he did work at silence and undelivered messages that year, and he did give *Putnam's* "Bartleby the Scrivener," published in 1853.

The mask through which Melville speaks in the story is that of a decent, pragmatic, elderly Wall Street lawyer (who prac-tices not far from Melville's boyhood neighborhood, and the Custom House, from which he retired in 1885). He is proud to work for robber barons, he tells us; he is as different from the copyist, or scrivener, Bartleby, as seems possible. And yet, like Bartleby, he is a victim of politics: As he has lost work as Mas-ter of Chancery because administrations changed, so Bartleby has lost a position, we learn, for similar reasons. Bartleby comes to haunt the lawyer and his chambers; Turkey and Nippers, matching opposites, strike the motif of doubleness for the story, and it soon becomes clear that something in these opposites, the narrator and his scrivener, is also matched.

For against all wisdom, not to mention sound business prac-tices, Bartleby is kept on, in spite of his refusal to work ("I would prefer not to"), as if the narrator required his presence. It seems that just as Melville finds his mask in the narrator—it is at this time that a campaign of family and friends fails to yield

Melville a diplomatic appointment by officials in the new administration of President Franklin Pierce—so the narrator finds *his* darker self in Bartleby. Quite like Bartleby, who ends up dead, "his face towards a high wall," the narrator has chambers on Wall Street that "looked upon the white wall of the interior of a spacious sky-light shaft" at one end, and, at the other, upon "a lofty brick wall." Like Bartleby (who is described, once, as "my fate"), he is in a blind alley of his life, and he looks upon "dead" walls.

In some ways, then, Melville writes not only of existential traps but of the need to cope with or create or accede to the presence of metaphors of one's interior being. He is speaking of aspects of the consciousness that makes fiction—the creation of alternate, mirroring selves—and it is selfish, needful, cunning, self-pitying, and sometimes even generous.

Bartleby, who starved away from an intolerable world—perhaps on behalf of the narrator, who had digested too much of it—had been a clerk "in the Dead Letter Office in Washington." His narrator, lamenting Bartleby and humanity, but probably also Herman Melville, speculates on "Dead letters! does it not sound like dead men?" He considers what dead letters might carry—pardon, hope, good tidings—and concludes that "on errands of life, these letters speed to death." For *life*, also read *fiction*.

Published by Harper & Brothers into the mid-1850s, Melville also read *Harper's Magazine*, renewing his subscription in 1852. And it was in *Harper's* that Charles Dickens's *Bleak House* was published serially in the United States, from April 1852 to October 1853. There's little reason to doubt that Melville saw those issues, including the issues of June and July 1852 containing the chapters (10 and 11) called "The Law-Writer" and "Our Dear Brother." In them, a man is portrayed so that, for the plot's sake, he might die. He is very much about paper and pen and, like Bartleby (at one point described as "folded up like a huge folio"), is a parody of Melville's profession; I suggest that Melville was moved by him indeed.

The law copyist, or scrivener, lives in Cook's Court, near Chancery Lane. (Remember that Bartleby's employer was Master of Chancery and that, well into the mid-twentieth century, America's Wall Street was the equivalent of England's legal Inns.) The man who copies legal documents in *Bleak House*, Melville would have read, calls himself "Nemo, Latin for no one." An advantage cited about Nemo is "that he never wants to sleep"; he is a haunted man. His landlady says, "They say he has sold himself to the Enemy," the Devil; he is "black-humored and gloomy" and lives in a tiny room "nearly black with soot and grease, and dirt"; his desk is "a wilderness marked with a rain of ink." "No curtain veils the darkness of the night," but Nemo's shutters are drawn; "through the two gaunt holes pierced in them, famine might be staring in. . . ." The filthy, ragged copyist, a figure of total despair, lies dead in his squalid room, the victim of an overdose of opium.

Melville, I suggest, read about Nemo before he wrote his story of Wall Street. He made Nemo his own, though he was drawn to him, I think, because the combination of despair, cruel laws, alienation, copying out and that "rain of ink" were irresistible. (Note how few writers, especially younger ones, can resist the lures of that tale.) Bartleby turns his face to a dead wall because he cannot tolerate his life. In the Dickens, it is a broken heart, a lost history, a condition in life that is denied by the scrivener. In the Melville, the man who copies dispositions according to common law, the law of human precedent, it is human life itself that is denied. Dickens, when he drew his copyist in *Bleak House*, was angry at conditions in English life; Melville, under Dickens's influence, saw his soul as "grated to pieces" by the great chore of living.

"The Encantadas or Enchanted Isles," published in *Putnam's* in 1854, appeals to the contemporary sensibility as much as "Bartleby" or "Benito Cereno." Although these are long stories, or novellas, they were written for magazine publication and are necessarily concise. The energy that comes of such compression, coupled with Melville's darkening vision and sexual and economic desperation—a third child was born in 1853, a fourth in 1855—results in a fiction that is grim (or effortfully funny, like "The Happy Failure" or "I and My Chimney," also published in 1854), a fiction that appropriates wild symbology from the romance (for example, a tortoise on the back of which is emblazoned a memento mori), and the mythic, fablelike qualities one associates with certain contemporary writers.

The Encantadas are the Galápagos Islands, "cinders dumped here and there in an outside city lot," Melville calls them. They are described as a Waste Land in the seas, where natural life is cruel and the human life that drifts in even crueller. Instead of chapters, we have ten sketches; there is no central character, and no single story. The islands become a matrix for authorial consciousness, a repository for attitude and mood. They are metaphors that link Melville's somber music, which describes an island as "tumbled masses of blackish or greenish stuff like the dross of an iron-furnace," yielding "a most Plutonian sight." This is a suite about hell, the outer, physical hell that is analogue to a sad man's interior hell—that, say, of the man who had, in discussing *Moby-Dick*, mentioned "the hell-fire in which the whole book is broiled." These sketches, from the former travel and adventure writer, offer a Swiftian scorning song about men who are more like dogs, and about islands that are more like ideas. If there is anyone heroic or admirable, it is Hunilla, of Sketch Eighth, who, abandoned on an island, endures her husband's and brother's deaths, and years of torture, to be seen, at the story's end, riding "upon a small gray ass . . ." and eyeing "the jointed workings of the beast's armorial cross." When Melville, the unbeliever, finds a character heroic, that character is often Christ-like, and is crucified with rapidity.

It is noteworthy that in describing an apocalyptically ugly wilderness like the Encantadas, Melville called them "cinders" and described them as a waste product of industry. Like all sensitive men and women of his time, and as a former sailor and a farmer, he was aware of the cruel encroachments of industrial process upon the countryside. His *Harper's* story of 1855, "The Tartarus of Maids," is often read as an attack upon nineteenth-century industrial despoliations. It is that, surely. But it is equally concerned with sexuality, and with fiction, and is as much about isolation and long silence as "The Encantadas."

The stories of this period, when examined in their collection, *The Piazza Tales* (1856), abound in vertical images, phallic shapes—lightning rods, masts, chimneys, and the high building that houses "The Paradise of Bachelors" in the story that was published along with "The Tartarus of Maids." As characters in "Bartleby" were paired, the two stories here are paired, the Pickwickian "Bachelors," the Dantean "Maids." The number nine—does Melville think of the Ninth Circle of Hell?—is echoed in each: nine carefree bachelors dine, and paper production in "Maids" takes nine minutes. We might remember that the nine months of gestation were significant to Melville at around this time.

So, in "Bachelors," the men dine at the top of a high building in London. They eat and drink in great quantity, are courtly to one another, and are "a band of brothers," with "no wives or children to give an anxious thought." Melville is stating his dream of freedom from the domestic responsibilities that stalk him (and which he cannot easily meet); he also expresses his desire to be free of the sexuality that, his fiction demonstrates, he copes with uneasily: It is Apollonian youth, or bachelor brothers, who most please his personae. Here, the men take snuff together from a silver goat's horn; they remove the snuff, which they will stuff into themselves, by "inserting . . . thumb and forefinger into its mouth." Melville goes to some length to create images that have to do with orifices and infantile pleasure. The bachelors are boys, and their aim is self-gratification, which exists in opposition to the cycles of biology represented in "The Tartarus of Maids," a story that's a matching opposite to "The Paradise of Bachelors," and another Melville tale of the underworld.

To enter that story's world, one enters a woman's body at her loins—the "Dantean gateway" at "the Black Notch" in a "Plutonian" hollow called "the Devil's Dungeon" that leads to "Blood River." Melville employs gothic images of ruined and decaying structures past which we are led to a paper mill. So we are dealing with female biology, male fear of it, hell, gothic terror, and paper.

Our narrator tells us that he is a "seedsman," that when the seeds he mails out are in paper folded into envelopes—he has come to buy more paper—the packets of seeds "assume not a little the appearance of business-letters ready for the mail." And we are back to letters, dead letters, the fiction that constitutes Melville's correspondence with the world.

The story starts out in whiteness, the menacing whiteness of Moby-Dick, for all is white vapor, the snow of January, the white walls of the mill, the paper itself. In a factory scene that Kafka might have envied and that Dickens could have written, the narrator confronts this sight: "At rows of blank-looking counters sat rows of blank-looking girls, with blank, white folders in their blank hands, all blankly folding blank paper." It is an industrial nightmare, and a writer's nightmare—especially if he is compelled to write because of inner need, or economics, or both.

If the writer thinks of the mailing out of seeds as, at once, an artistic need, an economic coercion, an expense of spirit, and an invitation to the production of babies who whip the cycle of responsibility round again, he might at this point tie the paper and seed images to the sexual toils he escaped in "Paradise" and slunk through at the Eve's opening of "Tartarus." Melville does. In the very next paragraph, we get "some huge frame of ponderous iron, with a vertical thing like a piston periodically rising and falling upon a heavy wooden block. Before it—its tame minister—stood a tall girl, feeding the iron animal with half-quires of rose-hued notepaper. . . ."

Thus, animal or biological pistoning—the act of sex itself—and the ceaseless sexual cycle our narrator (and Melville) cower before, becomes an "iron animal," a force that cannot be resisted—and it is a product of nature and of thinking man. The paper it prints bears a wreath of roses, like the frightening birthmark on the pink cheek in Hawthorne's story. Cruel scythes cut paper (as cruel saws have made stumps of the trees in the valley), paper pulp is a white river suspiciously sperm- and egglike as it flows into a room "stifling with a strange, bloodlike abdominal heat."

In the confusion of biology and writer's imagination, writer's need and domestic requirements, in the final room of the production process (it is presided over, as if a delivery room, by a woman who was a nurse), the narrator speculates about what could come to be written on all the blank paper he sees. These ruminations evoke those of the narrator of "Bartleby," for he considers "love-letters, marriage certificates, bills of divorce, registers of births, death-warrants"—much, in other words, that might have been on Melville's mind; these documents are the skeleton of what he works at. And then the narrator cites Locke and his comparison of the human mind at birth to a blank sheet of paper—at which point the writer is not only harassed breadwinner but a mother as well, since his writings are babies as much as babies become the world's blank paper to be scribbled upon.

"Time presses me," the seedsman puns as he leaves: It makes him jump to its bony tune, but it also writes his history upon his own soul. He speaks as all men—the "Ah, humanity!" of "Bartleby"—and as the writer, printed upon even as he imprints his inventions on paper, wraps his seeds (both art and life), and mails them out, hoping for mail in response.

If these are stories of the interior Melville, perhaps the triumph of this period is "Benito Cereno" (1855), a story that is very much about externalities—or seems to be. Like "Bartleby," "Benito Cereno" excites great writing by Melville, and, like "Bartleby," it suggests that the obvious is really enigma.

It is 1799, and an American merchantman, commanded by Captain Delano, lies near an island off Chile. The sea is "gray," the swells "lead," the sky "gray"; the "gray" fowl fly through "troubled gray vapors," and the scene is summarized by "Shadows present, foreshadowing shadows to come." So the reader is alerted that he will have to read this world and interpret the grays. He is further warned that what he sees are shadows; what casts them is hidden, and the reader must peer: The story is an exercise in, and an essay about, dramatic irony. As much as the subject is slavery and revolution, it is also perception and invention; it is about fiction, the successes and failures and tactics of which are very much on Melville's mind.

Delano is described from the start as having a "singularly undistrustful good-nature," and is virtually incapable of "the imputation of malign evil in man." From the start, Melville wants us to know that Delano misreads the world. So he resorts to the language of gothic romance. The slave ship looks like a "monastery after a thunder storm"; figures aboard her resemble "Black Friars pacing the cloisters"; the vessel is reminiscent of "superannuated Italian palaces" and her galleries evoke "tenantless balconies hung over the sea as if it were the grand Venetian canal." Delano is placed among the settings in which virgins are pursued by fright figures, and he should be at home—for he is, in terms of the evil and cruelty that Melville wishes to note, quite virginal.

Gothic conventions not only easily signal fright—we may perceive them; Delano cannot—but can serve to remind us at every turn that dying Europe, the worst of it, encounters the most naïve and imperceptive rawness of the New World. Apocalyptic thoughts bring out the best in Melville, who swims in them as in the sea. So we have such poetry about a ship as "while, like mourning weeds, dark festoons of sea-grass slimily swept to and fro . . . with every hearse-like roll of the hull."

Messages do not get through. And so Delano, maddeningly, scarily, cannot overcome his racism and innocence and see past the virtual *tableaux vivants* arranged for his benefit by the rebel slaves under Babo. The clues that strike us at once are misinterpreted in multiples by Delano. And then the awful symbol, in a story rife with symbols—puzzling rope knots, razors at throat—is uncovered. The ship's figurehead is revealed to be a human skeleton, that of a partner in the slave ship. And we are warned by Melville that what seem to be *only* symbols may be representations of what's actual, that language carries a cargo of the real, and that fiction is a matter of life and death.

The story slips without faltering into another convention, the "true" document that creates verisimilitude (as in the case of Captain Gulliver's deposition or, closer to home, Poe's "MS. Found in a Bottle," or Hawthorne's "discovery" of *The Scarlet Letter* manuscript). The statement by Benito Cereno, a seeming transcript, gives the European account of the slave rebellion, suggests to us how complicated and multifold any actuality is—how difficult to comprehend or relate—and serves to supply small, shuddery details. So we see, for example, that the original figurehead had been a wooden Christopher Columbus; the discoverer (as he was then thought to be, of course) of the New World is replaced by the Old World's grinning corpse: Slavery becomes the emblem of an inescapable fact—that we are haunted by our past, that the New Eden is not free of the old evils, that, as Melville complained to Hawthorne, "the malicious Devil is forever grinning in upon me."

A brief third section follows Cereno's testimony. It contains warnings inferred by Melville (and so many others) concerning the social conditions that will ignite the Civil War. It also offers another, a larger and historical, way of examining the events of the story. And it reminds us how, throughout the first part, we saw menace between the slave Babo and his master (then prisoner) Cereno, while Delano saw affection. Delano saw mastery, and we saw captivity. When Benito Cereno's "symbol of despotic command" is examined, it is seen not to be a sword, "but ghost of one," its scabbard "artificially stiffened." Melville does not, I think, speak here only of command, but of men seen as joined by affection who are later revealed to be acting in reversal of their customary relationships (the more powerful obeys, the slave commands). Melville joins notions of political power and emotional liaison, and not only to warn us that slaves rise up. The metaphor works in reverse as well, I think, and we are instructed that lovers are slaves and masters, that men can be unmanned by love (the limp scabbard), and can, as in the case of wan Don Cereno, even die of it.

The warning note is sounded again as Delano points to a sky he names as "blue," but which Cereno cannot acknowledge; to him, it is the gray, perhaps, of the story's opening. The shadows of that early passage are pointed at again as Delano says, "You are saved: what has cast such a shadow upon you?" Cereno answers, "The negro," and so warns a society of its sin and then its price—only then are we told of the empty scabbard—and points as well to Babo, who took Cereno's soul in partial payment for his freedom. The shadow is national, cultural, and also particular: Cereno dies, as did his partner.

Babo is the genius of the story—compare his invention, his gift for creating a shipwide fiction, to Delano's good dullness—

and his head, "that hive of subtlety," is taken from his body. It is his brain the white men fear. He is further reduced by this barbarism, and yet he becomes more of a threat. He stares at the white man from the post on which his head is impaled. He stares at the Old World and the New Eden, at unmanned Cereno, at church and monastery, storyteller and reader. And he stares them down. He began as a man and became a curse. And *his* message, for some, gets through.

And now we need to move ahead, through Melville's writing and nonwriting lifetime. Hawthorne, whom Melville loved and lost, has risen. He is America's second most powerful diplomat, the consul to Liverpool. (He was also Franklin Pierce's Bowdoin friend, and the author of his campaign biography.) Melville, failing at his novels and his efforts to achieve diplomatic appointment, suffering physically, his novel *Israel Potter* (1855) having been launched, only to sink, contracts for *The Confidence Man* having been signed, was sent in 1856, with his father-in-law's money, on a sea voyage that might bring him back to health and ease. He went to Liverpool, where he visited Hawthorne, who noted that Melville said he had "pretty much made up his mind to be annihilated." It is possible that Melville meant that he was faithless and was reconciled to a death with no afterlife. It is also possible to read the statement as a premonition of death. And it is not difficult, given Melville's state of mind, and his choked-off relationship with Hawthorne, to read the statement as a threat of suicide.

We might keep the possibility in mind as we move ahead to Melville's acceptance, in 1866, of a post at the Port of New York Custom House at Gansevoort Street, not far from his birthplace. In Boston and Salem, Hawthorne had begun his career at such a place; Melville would conclude his here. But he wrote his Civil War poems, and he went on to write the long poem *Clarel*, and, probably between the time of his retirement as a customs inspector in 1885 and his death in 1891, he worked on a poem that became the ballad "Billy in the Darbies" ("Billy in Irons"), which sparked a short novel—it concludes with the ballad and begins as a headnote to it—that we know as *Billy Budd, Sailor (An Inside Narrative)*.

We know a good deal about the composition of the novel because of the heroic work of Harrison Hayford and Merton M. Sealts, Jr. They show us, for example, that Melville worked through stages of imagining. First, there was the poem, about a sailor who was to be hanged for plotting a mutiny. Then came Melville's further interest in Billy in the context of the eighteenth-century British navy's concern with mutiny as a threat to fleetwide order. Claggert, Billy's nemesis, was born in further reworkings and then was made more complex, as is true of Captain Vere. The more Melville worked at this (apparent) first fiction in years, the more he thought about the nature of fiction, and the more he sought to deepen (and darken) his characters.

Surely he did mean much of the allegorizing that readers in the classroom parade before one another. Billy, impressed from the merchant, *Rights-of-Man*, does, after all, cry out "good-bye to you too, old *Rights-of-Man*." Vere does, after all, stand for verity. Billy, as he is hanged, does die as sun shoots through clouds to create "a soft glory as of the fleece of the Lamb of God seen in mystical vision." Melville does liken Claggert to Satan ("the scorpion for which the creator alone is responsible"). And he does liken Billy much to Adam as well as to Christ. Vere, who we are told cannot help but enforce the laws, must hang Billy for killing Claggert, even if the punishment is not fair—for it is just. Billy blesses Vere, we are reminded as we are told that *Billy Budd* is Melville's fiction of reconciliation: Left unfinished at his death, it is there to tell us that Melville has accepted fate's cruelty and his own cruel fate.

I would suggest, however, that the novel sustains Melville's preoccupation with fiction, that it creates dark characters for his sane madness, and that he is equally concerned with the mail getting through, and with his participation, to whatever degree, in a suicide.

Melville was a stern and difficult father and, when he wrote, he was removed, cranky, impatient, and selfish. We know little of his particular relationship with his son Malcolm, who in 1867 was eighteen years old. We do know that Malcolm was his first-born, and that he owned a pistol. Roistering one night after work at an insurance office run by his uncle's brother-in-law, he returned home very late, and he didn't emerge from his room the next day. That evening, Melville forced the door, to find that his son was dead. He had shot himself in the temple—an accident, the Melvilles insisted. What part the troubled father and husband played, or thought he played, in the suicide we cannot know.

But if we read *Billy Budd* with suicide and parental guilt in mind, and in just proportion, interesting considerations arise. Dansker, the voice of insight among the characters in the novel, calls him *Baby* Budd. The Mutiny Act, which necessitates Billy's death, is described as "War's child," which "takes after the father." In the next chapter, Captain Vere is described as "old enough to have been Billy's father." And so, when Billy goes to his death crying, "God Bless Captain Vere!" it is as if a father is exculpated by a son whom, because of man's laws and God's dispositions, he is required to sentence to death. It is possible that some of the electricity of the Vere-Budd relationship is the result of the father-son analogy that subconsciously galvanized Melville into writing the novel.

In this, another tale of shipboard levels of and kinds of perception, Melville is again obsessed with silence, as well as with ways of telling the truth. Billy, "under sudden provocation of strong heart-feeling," stutters "or even worse." The "even worse" is his choked agony of silence when, falsely accused by

Claggert, he cannot speak and, lashing out, kills his accuser. It is silence that leads to Billy's death, and it is silence—the failure of mail to get through—that still haunts Melville. I see little reconciliation here. He still quarrels with silence, and—remember the serpent "for which the creator alone is responsible"—he still quarrels with God.

But Melville, too, is a creator. He thinks hard of that for which he's responsible. So in Chapter 2, he worries about the form and function of his art, discussing Billy—"he is not presented as a conventional hero"—and his story, which "is no romance." He is speaking of what's actual, I think he says here, not of the symbolic. His subject, he tells us, really is death and silence and inexorable laws. In chapter 11, making Claggert an Iago, he worries that he errs in the direction of the gothic, or that his reader will, and he discusses "realism" and "Radcliffian romance." Chapter 13 reminds us that profound passion can be enacted "among the beggars and rakers of the garbage"; he is worrying about the effectiveness of his writing tactics; the ways of fiction are very much on his mind. In chapter 28, toward the novel's end (and his), he all but declaims or apologizes: "Truth uncompromisingly told will have its ragged edges; hence the conclusion of such a narration is apt to be less finished than an architectural finial." As he writes about Billy and Captain Vere and Claggert and Dansker, he writes about how he writes.

In 1851, Melville wrote to Hawthorne: "I have come to regard this matter of Fame as the most transparent of all vanities." Now, more than thirty years later, writing of Vere's end, he may speak of his deepest self: "The spirit that . . . may yet have indulged in the most secret of all passions, ambition, never attained to the fulness of fame." But I do not think he meant widespread notice to be his primary aim, any more than he meant riches when he complained about the earnings from his work. He was speaking, I would submit, about the ways in which the world could demonstrate to Melville—to any writer—that his work had been read and that it had made some difference. He was speaking of most earnest correspondence.

And there is Melville, who wants the mail to go out and to be delivered as much as he wants to receive it. He is riding in the stagecoach that carries the mail. At way station after way station, horses are changed, coaches are changed, the freight and mail and passengers roll on toward the end of the day. Melville writes to Hawthorne: "Lord, when shall we be done changing?" He sighs, in the corner of the stagecoach, in the corner of his life, "Ah, it's a long stage, and no inn in sight, and night coming, and the body cold."

THE RUB

In Colonial America, nutmegs were sometimes pur-
chased as charms, but they were mostly prized for seasoning.
Then, as now, cooks grated the fruit's hard stone in search of
sensual quickening of the bland, the thick, the sweetly heavy on
the tongue, the mucilaginous in the mouth. Herman Melville, in quest of both a charm and the soul's quickening,
sought among other things the devotion of Nathaniel
Hawthorne. At the time, Melville was finishing what he
would call *Moby-Dick*, he was getting in the corn and potato
crops on his Pittsfield farm, and he felt failed, poor, and cursed
as a writer. He was neither bathed in comfort nor seized by
joy: His heart was wakened only by what he called "the blackness of darkness beyond." On 1 June 1851, he wrote to
Hawthorne:

> Dollars damn me; and the malicious Devil is forever
> grinning in upon me, holding the door ajar. . . . I
> shall be worn out and perish, like an old nutmeg
> grater, grated to pieces by the constant attrition of
> the wood, that is, the nutmeg.

Melville's lament sounds familiar to us because we have vented
it, too. We are wearing away, we say. The cold, dull, spiceless
world grinds against us.

Because I'm stupider than Melville, *I* would have complained that the writer was the nutmeg, and the world the im-
plement for shaving from it bits of living skin. And I wonder if
others might be nearly as dumb as I. Wouldn't others have
thought that, too: that writers—the source, the meat, the
writerly point of it all, after all—allow their essence, their, well,
nuttiness, to be used? We sacrificial scribblers use it ourselves,
on purpose, until we're worn to little brown-gray nubbins. Isn't
that why, periodically, we demand and fail to find a different
life?

Yet Melville, mad and maddened—maybe wooing Hawthorne, but surely, like the rest of us, at least in search of an
ear at which to whine—chose to state the image in reverse of
expectations. In his formulation, the *artist* is the grater; the
nutmeg wears the grater away; and the instrument used to shave
off pieces—in this case, the writer—is what gets made dull,
and weak, and is broken at the last. Weaned on the Romantics
and accustomed to the self-regarding stare and uninflected
voice of a lot of our writers—sorrow is their game, and self is
both their names—most of us continue to think of the artist as
what is consumed by the world. Melville reminds us that the
world is our business, and that if we get used up, it's in the
course of tearing, hacking, and grinding at the thick rotundity
of earth.

When we're done, Melville implies (and so does *Moby-Dick*), the world survives both our attack and our need to make more of it, in our image or metaphor, than we found. We, grating, are worn down.

Writers are driven like Captain Ahab to their assault. They are compelled by the talent that possesses them—dues they have to pay for gifts they didn't request—to work away at the world. Some of us who have little talent, or none, are lured by the adulation in which writers are said (by those who do not know) to bask, or the fact that writers seem to have glamorous lives: yes, the thrill of rising at 5:30 A.M. and writing in the dark cold, or typing late at night after jobs that eat our hearts and livers, because no one will rescue us.

For some, or all, or combinations of these reasons, writers are strangers; we are spies. We dress like the others, and we speak their tongue. We want them to love us, to give us the correct change in their shops, and to hire us to teach too many sections of composition for too little pay. Yet, try as we do—and most of us try most of the time—we cannot stay loyal. We are undercover, working against their world. We want to set Diane Sawyer's dress on fire with lighted pages of *TV Guide*—not sit, for an hour or more, and *read* it, as though what it says matters. Moreover, we want to steal from the world the image of someone who, in all innocence and harmless satisfaction, *does* sit with *TV Guide* to learn whether Richard Caruso wears a toupee. We want to take that reader—who has done us no harm, and to whom we are *not* superior, smug as our ability to sketch him makes us feel—and we want to kidnap him into a novel or story or poem, maybe a patronizing essay.

But that reader is not stupid. First of all, what we hope might be untrue, even as we start to write, he knows *for certain:* That he will never, ever, read a word we invent. Furthermore, he understands our desires, if not our motives or needs. Writ-

ers are dishonest, he feels. There is something about us of the
shoplifter, the furtive taker in disguise, the Artful Dodger come
of age. We want something of him, or of his, and we will not tell
him outright what it is. So we make conversation with him—
the sort of phony person-of-the-people talk, with its verbal-
ized pauses and lapses of grammar that a sweaty professional
man employs while, say, watching someone who really knows
something change his tire or jump-start his car. We conde-
scend, and the *TV Guide* fellow realizes it. But he doesn't know
why. All he knows is that we make him uneasy—and he wants
us away from him.

If we are his colleagues and peers, he resents us even more.
Because he knows full well, then, what it is we want—he reads
the books of others, and he perhaps even teaches them; he has
some slight acquaintance with what artists do, and he doesn't
like them because he thinks they think they're better than he.
He is right. They are wrong, but it doesn't stop them—or
should I say us?

If he's reading *TV Guide* behind his text by Foucault, the
problem is compounded: He doesn't want us, or anyone else, to
know what he does, because he understands that we understand
that what people do is a metaphor for who they are, and that the
writer just might figure him out and, worse, say it memorably
and, even worse, that someone else might read what the writer
has said. If he's a book reviewer, ditto, though maybe with less
malice and a *touch* more incompetence folded in.

In other words, we are the enemy. And he, with *TV Guide*,
is part of the reality that is the nutmeg. He knows us: We're
what grates on him.

But, because he, in spite of his reading habits, understands
Melville better than we do, he also comprehends *TV Guide*,
and trays for making obscene ice-cube shapes, and beer that
hasn't beer in it, and electronically powered water guns shaped
like terrorists' weapons, and men who flail babies to death

against walls, and soldiers who crush the Constitution in their fists in order, they say, to preserve it. What's more, our reader understands that *these* are the world and that they and it will be here long after our metaphorical niceties and linguistic harmonies have been used for doorstops, fish wrap, and food for the hogs.

And we know that he knows. Yet we continue, as Melville did, to grind and grind and grind, hoping to chip and then shape, because we (like he) are compelled from the birth of consciousness to grate for our philosophical satisfaction, and our ordering needs, and for the illusion we harbor of glory.

In that same 1851 letter, Melville goes on to complain: "What I feel most moved to write, that is banned—it will not pay. Yet, altogether, write the *other* way I cannot. So the product is a final hash, and all my books are botches." Melville knew about both ways of writing: that which paid, and that which surely didn't. What his publishers and reading public and booksellers and reviewers wanted were the earlier books— popular combinations of adventure tale and travel narrative like *Typee*.

Melville was not only crazy enough to go on writing but also crazy enough to write what he knew would not pay. He was split between his need to do what reviewers, publishers, and readers wanted him to and his more ferocious need to do what he had to. He was not only the secret agent of dark, wild literature; he was the enemy—the grater of the nut—within his own mind and body. Driven to work, he worked against his own best interests. Needing money, he lamented it, scrounged and borrowed it, sought payment for his work—and yet refused to write what would bring the money in.

He was like me and most other writers. We all wish that we could write *Love's Flaring Nostrils* under a pseudonym, sell a million copies, then retire to write what we know we really must. But we cannot. Something that is part of the gift is also a compulsion: that we seek the darkness, not the light; that we serve up grindings of glass in blood sauce rather than the Fifth Avenue soufflé most readers want. We hope for cash; we sell, if at all, for too little; and we end up with everyone's scorn.

Let me say that I have had wonderful editors—literary and brilliant—and I know many like them who have risked much to publish real writing. Yet I still believe what I say here, as a general truth: Do you think that most editors and the houses for which they work are really interested in the blackness of darkness beyond? How can an editor or publisher be interested in anything other than selling books? Doesn't the editing process, sweet and advisory as it may seem, reinforce the notion that nonprofit books about being nutmeg graters are of little interest to the world of what are called "books"? Editors must sell, and so most of them try to help us—yes, they are wise and smart and gentle; no, they aren't whores—to make the book's appeal a bit more broad: which means making it inviting to the guy with *TV Guide* beside him at the kitchen table in a house we would seek, at much cost, to avoid living in. If the book is not to be reshaped to that man's standards, then often enough it is rejected before editing can begin.

In other words, we write against hope in the hope that what we write will be bought by those who shop in the hope that what they'll buy and publish will not be what we write. And, somehow, nevertheless, men and women of wit and goodwill publish what we write, hoping against hope that the book they know can't be sold still might sell. Each hope, and every such transaction, is a nudge of the writer's consciousness in the direction of the nut, and away from the disintegration of the grater.

Is there any better lesson for a writer than that of being published and then sold (or not)? It teaches us all how much a part of the world the writer really is.

* * *

So we grate not only at the world, which rubs us, wears us, and frays us, making us more like it: We grind at *ourselves.* We—surely of the world (and never as far from it in spirit as our self-imposed and world-willed exile might suggest at first)—are the nutmeg, and we are the grater, as well.

When we write about us, therefore, we are writing of the world. And when we complain, I would suggest, we are celebrating at the same time. The authentic cry of the self, it seems to me, is also a celebration of reality's wonders. It may not be gleeful—ecstasy need not be fun—but it is *not* a disappearance into mere language. Nor is good writing a kind of showing off, a cri de coeur essentially heartless, a pirouette of the pencil in the artful half-light of an office where someone else picks up the rent. That sort of bad writing is either the fancy dancing of language insisting that the writer is the story or it is the imitation of exhaustion that we associate with languid lingerie models in gleaming magazines—not the evocation of the genuine striving that exhausts.

No one complained longer or louder than Melville, and no one failed in public more disastrously. His driven Ahab in *Moby-Dick*, as monomaniacal as his author and surely his author's mask, is pictured like this:

> And have I not tallied the whale, Ahab would mutter to himself, as after poring over his charts till long after midnight he would throw himself back in reveries—tallied him, and shall he escape? His broad fins are bored, and scalloped out like a lost sheep's ear! And here, his mad mind would run on in a breathless race; till a weariness and faintness of pondering came over him; and in the open air of the deck he would

seek to recover his strength. Ah, God! What trances
of torments does that man endure who is consumed
with one unachieved revengeful desire. He sleeps
with clenched hands; and wakes with his own bloody
nails in his palms.

(chapter 44, "The Chart")

Ahab sees the whale as a lover might see his beloved, by drawing and redrawing the intimacies of the curve and hollow of fin.
The sheep he alludes to is "lost," and thus poignant—not
merely hunted and detested. And if Christ is a shepherd, and
also a lamb, then the hunter crucifies himself with his own nails.
God is part of man, man is partly God—or at least he functions
in God's manner, metaphorically—and what's hated and sought
is considered like a creature beloved. In the majesty of the
world, in the scallops of its madnesses, the pursuer and his artist
cannot exist independently of the ground their battle rages on.
Ahab's despair is a variety of glory.

One of the wonderful love stories of our time is *A Long and
Happy Life* (1962) by Reynolds Price. The novel opens with this
single sentence:

Just with his body and from inside like a snake, leaning that black motorcycle side to side, cutting in and
out of the slow line of cars to get there first, staring
due-north through goggles towards Mount Moriah
and switching coon tails in everybody's face was Wesley Beavers, and laid against his back like sleep,
spraddle-legged on the sheepskin seat behind him
was Rosacoke Mustian who was maybe his girl and
who had given up looking into the wind and trying to
nod at every sad car in the line, and when he even
speeded up and passed the truck (lent for the afternoon by Mr. Isaac Alston and driven by Sammy his

man, hauling one pine box and one black boy dressed in all he could borrow, set up in a ladder-back chair with flowers banked around him and a foot on the box to steady it)—when he even passed that, Rosacoke said once into his back "Don't" and rested in humiliation, not thinking but with her hands on his hips for dear life and her white blouse blown out behind her like a banner in defeat.

Many delights live in those living lines. It is the first and last time that Reynolds Price sounded like Faulkner; it is as good an image as I have read of a couple cemented by need and speed and gravity itself—she holds his hips "for dear life" while Wesley, racing away from biology and death, passes "even" the body bound for its burying, as Rosa (an insister upon what's natural, proper, and seemly) whispers only "Don't"—so that Price has summed his characters up in a single long breath. And it is a statement about what we, as bound and frightened lovers, can do: speed up, hold on, and endure. Rosacoke's whipped white blouse is "a banner in defeat." The novel is as much about losing as triumph. And so is life. And so, as you well know, is art. These contemporary lovers—arrested in Price's prose like the lovers on Keats's Grecian urn, forever in pursuit—are also rendered as people about whom we care: they will not, in their *lives*, Price tells us (and makes us want to know), resist time and sorrow and death. But in art they will. They are art's impassioned, frozen characters, given the illusion of sorrow and love, and made plausible to us.

Ahab, crazed by his pursuit of what he deduces or wishes could be found behind the blinding blankness of the palpable world, commands the Indian Tashtego to nail his captain's flag upon the *Pequod*'s mast. The bare arm slams its hammer; the crimson banner whips in the wind. Ahab grinds upon the nutmeg:

> I turn my body from the sun. What ho, Tashtego! let
> me hear thy hammer. . . . Oh, lonely death on lonely
> life! Oh, now I feel my topmost greatness lies in my
> topmost grief. . . . Towards thee I roll, thou all-
> destroying but unconquering whale; to the last I
> grapple with thee; from hell's heart I stab at thee; for
> hate's sake I spit my last breath at thee.
>   (chapter 135, "The Chase—Third Day")

Ahab is dragged to his death by the diving Moby-Dick. As the whale descends with Ahab's harpoon in him and Ahab coiled in the harpoon's line, the ship that Moby-Dick has shattered quickly sinks. Ishmael—the storyteller, the sole survivor, the voice compelled to bear witness to the magnificence of Ahab's (and Melville's) grinding at the universe—notes how a few inches of the mainmast protrude from the ocean's surface: "at that instant, a red arm and a hammer hovered backwardly lifted in the open air, in the act of nailing the flag faster and yet faster to the subsiding spar." It is a banner of a terrible anguish and a murderous defeat; and it is also, of course, heroic. The great shroud of the sea rolls over small and scratchy man, but he has demanded, hugely, his little time.

In Price's novel, Rosacoke's blouse is the flag of the artist's rendered world and of the actual world we celebrate as it maddens us. Our triumph is in understanding that we serve what we try to reinvent. Like real heroes, Wesley and Rosacoke carry our fear and our desire. They are emblems, but they seem ac-tual—*there's* artistic victory—as they fight for life while racing toward their death. The world on which they ride, the world in-side of which that truck-borne body will be rested, is what Price's heroine's banner finally celebrates. The *Pequod*'s crew has a ship for a coffin. Ishmael, the artist, survives by floating on his dear friend Queequeg's coffin. Price bears the coffin to us, and himself, on a pickup truck in the modern South. But that coffin's freight is the world, beneath whose waters the masts of the *Pequod* disappear as Ahab's flag flies one last failing time before the seas roll over it. And the same seas chew at the stones and soil of islands from whose tropical evergreens fall the small hard fruits of nutmeg, whose seeds we grate—as if we sprinkle grave dirt in our gardens—to taste the spice for which, caught in our lives, we yearn.

SUITORS BY BOZ

I

THE NARRATORS IN three of Charles Dickens's great novels—*David Copperfield, Bleak House,* and *Our Mutual Friend*—speak and write not only for and about themselves and their troubles but also for and about Dickens's emotional wounds. It is their purpose to beguile their audience, to persuade it of their own woundedness and thus win for themselves and for their author the sympathies of the reader. While these narrators cannot knit what is rent in Dickens, they do knit the act of writing to the state of sorrow, to Dickens's state of sorrow. David Copperfield, Esther Summerson, and Mr. Venus, the articulator of bones, appear before us as suitors: They woo.

Dickens's protagonist begins *David Copperfield* with a chapter entitled "I am Born." Being born is much of what this great novel is about, and chapter 64, which starts "And now my written story ends. I look back, once more—for the last time—

before I close these leaves," is as much about birth as the sentence with which the first chapter starts: "Whether I shall turn out to be the hero of my own life, or whether that station will be held by anybody else, these pages must show."

When Dickens says "must show," I think he means to demonstrate the imperative mood of his narrator, a middle-aged man who is a very successful novelist, lucky (at last) in love, surrounded by adoring family and friends—in short, the epitome of the middle-class fairy tale Dickens so often told. The novel is full of writers and references to writing, all of them relevant to Dickens, beginning with the initials of the protagonist, D. C., which reverse the author's C. D. David's aunt's friend, Mr. Dick, the former Richard Babley, is also a writer—he is always at work on his Memorial, a missive about the thoughts of the beheaded King Charles that incessantly invade his brain. The Dick, the Charles, the Babel or babble or Babley, the constant writing—all remind us again of our author. And Mr. Micawber speaks (like Dickens's father, John) as if writing formal letters, and he sets pen to paper with remarkable frequency. David's school-day friend, Traddles, writes legal documents, and his wife copies them. David's beloved schoolmaster, Dr. Strong, is writing a dictionary. And David, of course, is writing the book we read.

The novel is about writing. David Copperfield is *David Copperfield*. He is born as a character—"hero," "pages"—and he ends that way—"my story," "these leaves." And Dickens, who was required to end his monthly segments at climactic moments and still give the impression of artless pondering—of sincerity as opposed to artfulness—succeeds magnificently. Thus, David, the bewitched young schoolboy who watches tall, curly-haired, self-assured Steerforth fall asleep with "his handsome face turned up, and his head reclining easily on his arm," cannot know, though Dickens must, that when Steerforth dies (as justice demands) drowned and battered by the sea at the novel's end, the older and wiser David sees him "lying with his head upon his arm, as I had often seen him lie at school." The reader feels the satisfaction such symmetry lends to narrative, while David appears to stumble upon the repeated image. Dickens has his fictive cake as we devour it.

Among the lessons David learns at school during his enchantment by the irresistible Steerforth is that storytelling offers power. It is a power that Dickens loved. We can see it in the introductions to his novels—he calls *Copperfield* his "favourite child" in one—where he demonstrates that he needs to remain in touch with his readers, whom he loves to sway. We can see it also in his health-shattering, life-ending round of public readings, and in his refusal to give up the crushing schedule of his editing—he conducted magazines from about the time of *Copperfield* until his death. He rejoiced in influencing his audience.

So here is young Copperfield, delighting in his schoolboy crush, and here is his putative author, the older David Copperfield, looking back at his boyhood and telling us that "to disappoint or displease Steerforth was of course out of the question." Steerforth has noted David's ability to recall the stories he read in his precocious, lonely boyhood, and, being unable to sleep well, has commanded that David retell the stories to soothe his wakefulness and lull him to sleep. "We'll make some regular Arabian Nights of it," Steerforth says. He wakes David before dawn if he pleases, he keeps him up late if he must, and David recalls that "it was a tiresome thing to be roused, like the Sultana Sheherezade."

Steerforth has the erotic power to command David to awaken and tell his stories. But David has—he slowly learns this—the power to charm his sultan with his stories: at his book's end, he hears "the roar of many voices, not indifferent to me," and that fame is not unimportant to him, as self-effacingly as he tries to note it. The power signified by reputation is, I think, really the power of the storyteller. According to Dickens's description of the older David's description of the younger David's being "like the Sultana Sheherezade," the writer has the ability to defeat death. For Sheherezade had to entertain her lord, who was prepared to have her put to death if she failed to interest him.

In a novel about a writer, a novel in which the book is the man, Dickens does what all novelists do: He resists time by rowing backward, against the current, into his life. Like all serious artists, he takes the matter of his art as a matter of life and death. The writer, he believes, must succeed or die. Success, here, is characterized as successful wooing. Storytelling, to Dickens, is a making of love and a challenge to death. This is urgent business, and whether David is the hero of his life, these pages *must* show.

The novelist Dickens and the novelist Copperfield have spent their writing lives, as *Copperfield* opens, in contending with what David refers to as "a vague unhappy loss or want of something." He complains to Agnes, whom we know he should have married, that "I want some faculty of mind that I ought to have." He says then that the "old unhappy loss or want of something had, I am conscious, some place in my heart; but not to the embitterment of my life." And it is perhaps with that overmuch protestation about not being bitter that we recognize fully that Dickens the cunning novelist, in writing of the growth of his naïve, fictional writer, is working at a powerful rhetoric. His subtextual argument, as he writes of David's life with his lovely, dumb, incapable, darling wife, Dora, is generated by his stated feeling that he wished, "sometimes, for a little while," that "my wife had been my counsellor; had had more character and purpose, to sustain me and improve me by; had been endowed with power to fill up the void which somewhere seemed to be about me."

Dora is modeled after Dickens's wife, Kate, Catherine Hogarth, whom he would expel from his household and from her children after publicly humiliating her as he conducted his long affair with Ellen Ternan. Kate bore ten children and grew dumpy. Dickens has Dr. Strong's young wife, Annie, say, "There can be no disparity in marriage like unsuitability of mind and purpose," and I wonder if she might not speak for her author. Her *immediate* author, David, knows that he is caught in such a "disparity." He is an honorable man, and he will not abandon Dora, whom he believes himself to love in spite of herself. And she is as loving and cuddly as her lapdog, whose death prefigures hers.

She must of course die if David is to escape his marriage and come to his senses about Agnes, who is always more of a nurse and mother than flesh-and-blood woman (in spite of Uriah Heep's leering lust for her). But a nurse and mother seems to be what David requires—a "counsellor" to "sustain" and "improve" him. Yet he is as obliged, he feels, to Dora as Dickens must have felt obliged to Kate. Although the "old unhappy feeling pervaded my life . . . undefined as ever . . . like a strain of sorrowful music faintly heard in the night," he insists, "I loved my wife dearly, and I was happy," although "there was always something wanting."

So: "In fulfilment of the compact I have made with myself, to reflect my mind on this paper, I again examine it, closely." And here, in the light of an apparently spontaneous recollection, is the wily rhetoric Dickens fashions: "I always loved her. What I am describing, slumbered, and half awoke, and slept again, in the innermost recesses of my mind. There was no evidence of it in me; I know of no influence it had in anything I said or did. I bore the weight of all our little cares, and all my [writing] projects; Dora held the pens."

I think that Dickens addresses himself as his David addresses *him*self. The argument here is that of a middle-aged man whose wife had to die before he could be free to love someone else, or to act on that love. It is himself each writer addresses, the self that, like Steerforth, "slumbered, and half awoke, and slept again": the self who must be seduced by the story, the self whose approbation means life. It was Dickens's plan for *The Mystery of Edwin Drood*, which was half-completed when he died in 1870, to have the villainous John Jasper cross-examine himself in his jail cell, as if he were both interrogator and prisoner. That Freudian fissure in the self would have been a triumph, but I believe that something similar already exists in *David Copperfield* and other of Dickens's novels. Here is the novelist who writes a novel about a novelist who writes a book about his younger self. And in the fictional book, the fictional novelist performs the actual novelist's life-and-death errand: He works to assure himself that his life is not a penal sentence, that he is not culpable.

In this novel about writing and writers, there is much seduction. Steerforth seduces his mother's companion, Rosa Dartle, then—in a sense—David, and then Emily. Mr. Murdstone seduces David's young mother. Emily's friend Martha is seduced and becomes a prostitute. Aunt Trotwood was seduced by a ne'er-do-well when she was a girl. Sheherezade must, by way of her art, seduce her master into letting her live. And David (and his creator) must seduce his guilty self, relieved by having killed his wife off on "these pages," "these leaves," into believing that "I always loved her."

When Dora lies dying, therefore, it is *she* who calls for Agnes, who will replace her. It is she who instructs Agnes to marry her soon-to-be-widowed husband. It is she who instructs the grieving David, "Oh, Doady, after more years, you never could have loved your child-wife better than you do; and, after more years, she would so have tried and disappointed you, that you might not have been able to love her half so well! I know I was young and foolish. It is much better as it is!"

David is set free of the woman he married by mistake. And, of course, he eventually—after so very much obtuseness—

recognizes that it is Agnes whom he needs and loves. But before he does, he ponders his guilty heart. The narrative is in the present tense as Dora dies, so those moments of David's past mesh wonderfully with the moments during which he writes of that death: He thinks "with a blind remorse of all those secret feelings I have nourished since my marriage. . . . Would it, indeed, have been better if we had loved each other as a boy and a girl, and forgotten it? Undisciplined heart, reply!" That is Dickens speaking to Dickens as David recollects his youthful "blind remorse": What was *then* in David's life is *now* in the life of the middle-aged David and his author. And Dora's permission, in effect, for the *man* not to love his wife enough, her willingness to die away from him for the sake of his needs, is the tale with which David as Sheherezade seduces his auditor and judge: himself.

When Dora dies, Agnes descends the stairs from the deathbed and—David has always thought of her as poised on a staircase, against a window, as if a stained-glass figure—she surely enough points to heaven to announce Dora's death. At the novel's end, as the famous and contented fictional author finishes reviewing what is after all a haunted life, he invokes Agnes—surely it is *she* who is "the hero of my own life"?—and prays that she will "be by me when I close my life indeed" as he closes it in word. He prays that he may "still find thee near me, pointing upward!" In other words, he takes his comfort from having married an angel of death.

David was born six months after his father's death. His lovely and helpless mother—who bears no small resemblance to Dora—is soon enough married to the wonderfully named Mr. Murdstone (he is both *merde* and *murderer* of David's idyll with his mother). To facilitate her being wooed, or to save David the anxiety of Mr. Murdstone's presence, or because Mr. Murdstone requires it, Peggotty, David's beloved nurse, and Mrs. Copperfield decide that David is to go with Peggotty to see her family at Yarmouth. Peggotty, who is stout, embraces people emotionally and in consequence bursts buttons from her clothing. David wonders as they ride away from his mother "whether, if she were employed to lose me like the boy in the fairy tale, I should be able to track my way home again by the buttons she would shed."

He refers, of course, to the Hansel and Gretel story, in which parents deliberately abandon their children in the dangerous forest in order that what little food is available go to the elders. *David Copperfield* grew from Dickens's recollections of his abandonment by his parents, for about three months, while he, taken from school and set to work in a blacking factory, was forced to live alone in the tough and often frightening London of the time; the rest of the family, to save money, lived with John Dickens, imprisoned in the Marshalsea debtors' prison.

Dickens, provoked by a question from his friend, agent, and first biographer, John Forster, began an autobiography about those traumatic days, then left it and began *David Copperfield*, which uses the same emotional material. Indeed, speaking of the boys with whom he was forced to work in the dark and rat-infested cellar of the factory, both Dickens in the fragment and David in *David Copperfield* say: "No words can express the secret agony of my soul as I sunk into this companionship . . . and felt my early hopes of growing up to be a learned and distinguished man crushed in my breast." "It is wonderful to me how I could have been so easily cast away at such an age," Dickens writes in the autobiographical fragment; "it seems wonderful to me that nobody should have made any sign in my behalf," David writes.

And it is in David's and Dickens's writings that someone *does* make a sign on his behalf. Dickens's novels are filled with male and female fairy godmothers, from Mr. Brownlow of *Oliver Twist* to Jenny Wren, the little dressmaker of *Our Mutual Friend*, Dickens's last completed novel. And in *David Copperfield*, Agnes, ever sacred, replaces David's mother, supplants David's bothersome wife, and offers the sustenance and improvement, the "lack or want" of which David has always felt. I think she replaces Dickens's mother, too: When John Dickens was released from prison, and the family was reunited, Dickens said of his hated job: "I never afterwards forgot, I never shall forget, I never can forget, that my mother was warm for my being sent back."

So a child in the thrall of nightmare—Dickens is the great poet of children's terror—becomes a young man in a different nightmare. He and his author write their way out of their dreams so that David can conclude his book, "my life," "these pages," by referring to "the shadows which I now dismiss." In his novel about writing, Dickens through David addresses his darkest, most secret, and most urgent needs to "the reader whom I love," his very self.

II

IT MIGHT SEEM disloyal to actual women of talent and quirk if we were to read Charles Dickens's *Bleak House* and celebrate its co-narrator, Esther Summerson. She seems coy from beginning to end; she denigrates herself while telling us the story of her life from earliest memory to matronhood—insisting, that is, on commemorating her existence while at the same time demanding that we pay no attention.

"I know I am not clever," she says as she begins, in chapter 3, to tell her story. So powerful is her sense of not mattering, she says, that "I have a great deal of difficulty in beginning to write my portion of these pages." Yet she is compelled to write her life: "It seems so curious to me to be obliged to write all this about myself! As if this narrative were the narrative of *my* life!" Who or what obliges her, and whose voice shares the telling of the story, is never clear—is, indeed, a subsuming puzzle in this great novel of puzzlement. The one voice, omniscient and outraged, begins the book with its images of fog, gas, mud, and corruption—"a soft black drizzle with flakes of soot in it as big as full-grown snowflakes—gone into mourning, one might imagine, for the death of the sun"—and sustains it through the image of London's Holborn coated with "a thick, yellow liquor . . . offensive to the sight and more offensive to the smell," on to "where the straw-roofs of the wretched huts . . . are being scattered by the wind; where the clay and water are hard frozen, and the mill in which the gaunt blind horse goes round all day, looks like an instrument of human torture."

Esther shares the narrative with this angry voice and only once or twice shows a tentative anger of her own. The novel is about lying, pollution, physical and psychic disease, and incurable injustice. Esther is a victim of that injustice, as is almost everyone about whom she cares. Her first-person narrative, twined about the furious third-person narrative, gives us a sense of simultaneity: We see two aspects of corrupt England—the public and upper-class and juridical, on the one hand, and, on the other, the domestic, the young, the disenfranchised, the relenting.

We want to side with Esther, no matter her annoying self-dismissal: She is raised cruelly by a cold guardian, and is one more Dickensian orphan in the chiaroscuro world of adult Experience that crushes childish Innocence. He understood in such fairy-tale situations not only the dark charm for the reader in such victimizing but also the possibility for happy transformation. Of course these fairy tales threatened horrible change, and the children in them—the child in us—must first be terrorized and *then*, if ever, saved. But wish for Esther's triumph as we do, root for her as we must, we are distanced (if not offended) by the dialectic she quickly establishes in addressing us. She notes that she is somehow approved, then derides the approval. We feel that she unduly demands our response, and we punish her by withholding it. She is like a demanding child who insists she is undemanding. That Esther can summon these reactions in readers—approval, annoyance, a kind of angry, parental championing—suggests that Dickens has won through: He has made a character we cannot, one way and another, deny.

Here is Esther as she writes, apparently, to us: "I hope it is not self-indulgent to shed these tears as I think of it. I am very thankful, I am very cheerful, but I cannot quite help their coming to my eyes." She adds, "There! I have wiped them away now, and can go on again properly." The little sniff and smile of bravery have us gritting our teeth.

Esther and two other orphans, Ada and Richard, are cared for by John Jarndyce, this novel's fairy godmother. He is a party to *Jarndyce v. Jarndyce*, a contesting of wills that lasts seventy years, exhausts the estate in legal fees, and ruins the lives of those who are unwise enough to invest emotionally or financially in its outcome. He establishes Esther, Richard, and Ada in Bleak House, gives them security and love, and he names Esther: She is Dame Durden, Little Woman—she is a doll in a doll's house, one of Dickens's pocket women. The zest with which she takes to her role as diminutive mistress of Bleak House adds to the modern reader's itchiness. And here, then, is where we ought to see what composes the incessantly self-effacing "her" who, given the household keys, in effect the supervision of Bleak House, what is regarded by Ada as "the magnitude of . . . trust," replies *now*, in her maturity, all trials past and her heroism proved to the world, "I knew, to be sure, that it was the dear girl's kindness; but I liked to be so pleasantly cheated"—that is, benevolently lied to by Ada and Jarndyce about her competence.

Esther "was brought up, from my earliest remembrance—like some of the princesses in the fairy stories, only I was not charming—by my godmother." This woman is the sister of the haughty Lady Dedlock, who, as a girl, became pregnant by a soldier whom she loved and later thought dead. When she gave birth to Esther, she thought her child was dying; her repressive sister later told her that the child had died, but raised her— while Lady Dedlock turned her heart to ice to preserve her- self—in a grim, puritanical household. The unearthing to Esther of her secret history, and her mother's, by way of legal documents and dreadful lawyers, all tied to *Jarndyce v. Jarndyce*, is a marvel of plotting and detective work. In this novel, the world is a crime.

Esther's childhood is dark, church-dominated, and admin- istered by the godmother who "never smiled." The relationship fascinated Dickens, who created two other versions of it—a marvelous one in Miss Havisham and Estella in *Great Expecta- tions* and a less splendid but maybe more frightening one in Mrs. Clennam and her son Arthur in *Little Dorrit*. The child Esther of course feels the joyless distance her godmother cre- ates: "It made me very sorry to consider how good she was, and how unworthy of her I was." The result is not only anger—"I never loved my godmother as I ought to have loved her"—but also a compounded guilt: "I felt that I must have loved her if I had been a better girl."

On Esther's birthday ("the most melancholy day . . . in the whole year"),

> The clock ticked, the fire clicked; not another sound. . . . I happened to look timidly up from my stitching across the table, at my godmother, and I saw in her face, looking gloomily at me, "It would have been far better, little Esther, that you had no birthday; that you had never been born!"

That pronouncement is not spoken: Esther reads it in her god- mother's expression. She is conditioned to find her devaluation everywhere.

She weeps and looks for a reason for her valuelessness. She asks, "O, dear godmother, tell me, pray do tell me, did mama die on my birthday?" She is told no, instructed to ask no more, and receives no comfort; she is in the nightmare that, Dickens postulates again and again, is the habitat of childhood. The godmother moves to leave the room, and Esther becomes hysterical, crying of her mother: "What did I do to her? How did I lose her? Why am I so different from other children, and why is it my fault, dear godmother? No, no, no, don't go away. O, speak to me!" The godmother stands above the child, who is kneeling. Esther looks at her "darkened" face, puts "up my trembling little hand to clasp hers, or to beg her pardon with what earnestness I might, but withdrew it as she looked at me, and laid it on my fluttering heart."

As we witness this inhumanity, we may also witness in ourselves an aspect of the godmother's cruelty. If we are honest, we admit to a temptation also to turn away from this portrayal of this child. We are reacting to our realization that Esther is not merely recounting sorrow; she is writing "my portion of these pages." She wants us to see her frailty, to see her unreasonable guiltiness, to feel her hand, her *little* hand, tremble. Feel my heart, she says: It *flutters*.

Esther is, of course, creating a rhetoric. She wants to achieve something, and we are not certain what. But we feel it, and we feel therefore that her sincerity is called into doubt. Even when she confesses to us—"unless my vanity should deceive me (as I know it may, for I may be very vain, without suspecting it—though indeed I don't)"—we suspect the confession. *What is it you want?* we snarl.

Her godmother calls her "orphaned and degraded"; sending her away uncomforted, she adds, "Submission, self-denial, diligent work, are the preparations for a life begun with such a shadow on it. You are different from other children, Esther, because you were not born, like them, in common sinfulness and wrath. You are set apart." The grown-up Esther comments while recounting this scene: "I hope it is not self-indulgent to shed these tears as I think of it. I am very thankful, I am very cheerful, but I cannot help their coming to my eyes." She is the writer. She chooses what to include. If, recalling her awful childhood, she weeps, then she need not write down her weeping. But clearly she wants us to know that she has not healed. This is a book of ghosts: Lady Dedlock's manor house features a Ghost's Walk on which spectral footfalls are heard; landscapes in mist show "ghosts of trees and hedges"; a Dedlock cousin "parade[s] the mansion like a ghost." And Esther wants us to know that she is her own ghost: She haunts herself as she writes, and she wants us to feel the clammy breath of that haunting. For she is, despite her luck and courage and her present happy estate, still a tortured, small girl. As the third-person narrator seeks to persuade us with rage of the inhumanity of England in general, Esther seeks to persuade us of the small, particularized inhumanity of her suffering. She is like Catherine Earnshaw in *Wuthering Heights:* She scratches at the window, calling to us, "Let me in—let me in!"

This child, who lives in "a kind of fright beyond my grief," can confide only to her doll. Crying herself to sleep on her birthday night, she knows "that I had brought no joy, at any time, to anybody's heart, and that I was to no one upon earth what Dolly was to me."

The godmother dies, unrelenting, as Esther asks "for blessing and forgiveness" or—those failing—"the least sign that she knew or heard me." She is given nothing. Then, in her grief and to her astonishment, Esther's life is changed by John Jarndyce's benevolent machinations. She is to be sent to a school where she will be cared for, and even cared about, as she assists in the teaching. Before she leaves, she performs a ritual that she does not explain: "A day or two before [her departure], I had wrapped the dear old doll in her own shawl, and quietly laid her—I am half ashamed to tell it—in the garden-earth under the tree that shaded my old window."

Whenever Esther expresses shame to her reader, it is because she has focused attention on her own attention to her emotional needs for expression of sorrow, for self-assurance—not necessarily for the act itself that she describes so much as for *how* she describes it. She employs a rhetorical shame, then, that is about telling, not about what is told. She is a damaged child, and she needs to describe her damage. She wonders if we will listen. She *wants* us to listen. So she woos us as she writes her pages. And her motive lies in the resolution she made on her dreadfully ironic birthday night: "to try to be industrious, contented, and true-hearted, and to do some good to some one, and win some love if I could."

It is to win us over, to "win some love," that she fashions her narrative. Why, then, the burial of the doll, of her only confidante, who was to Esther what Esther was not allowed to be to anyone else? With a shovel, Esther demonstrates dramatically to herself that she is a dead child (as her mother thought), and that she must put her terrified childhood behind her; with her pen, she demonstrates to herself (grown older) and to us that what is buried may nevertheless rise up. And speaking for Dickens of his own anguished childhood that will not be laid, she is an artful—*not* naïve and spontaneous—writer. She is preparing us at the start of this immense novel for the conclusion of her story. Esther has designs.

As she and the omniscient narrator progress, a vast web of plot is created. When someone moves on it, say in an iron mill in the industrial north, strands shiver near an Inn of Court in central London. A law writer who named himself Nemo, *No One*, dies: He is Esther's father, Lady Dedlock's beloved, and he is—after burying himself in the suffocating English law while alive—buried in a crowded graveyard to which Lady Dedlock, getting wind of his identity, is taken by Jo, the ill, confused, and sad boy sweeper who is victimized by the injustice at which the novel thunders. Jo will spread disease from the low to the high, not sparing Esther, and all the insulated, sadly separate lives of the novel will be shown by Dickens to be linked by what the narrator, on the first page, calls "general infection."

A confusing element is introduced when the lawyer, Tulkinghorn, trying to identify who was seen in Lady Dedlock's clothing at the cemetery—he is protecting Lord Dedlock's name and station—causes Hortense, Lady Dedlock's maid, to wear her mistress's dress. Jo is then asked (with the reader in the dark) to identify the lady he led to the graveyard. Another element in the crowded plot is made up of two families of brick makers— impoverished, uneducated, brutal. Esther befriends the women and is present when one of them can only watch helplessly as the sick infant on her lap dies. Esther remembers Jenny as "the mother of the dead child," a term she repeats often in her narrative.

When Lady Dedlock is exposed by Tulkinghorn, she flees her husband and her honorable life, making it clear that she intends to die. But Lord Dedlock loves her unconditionally, and he sends Inspector Bucket and Esther after her. They follow a metaphor, asking after the dress, riding for miles in a frantic pursuit. Ultimately, they meet up with the brick makers, from whose number Jenny is missing. Vital hours are lost before Inspector Bucket realizes that Lady Dedlock paid Jenny to switch dresses with her: They have in reality been tracking Jenny in Lady Dedlock's dress while she, in Jenny's clothing, has walked, in mire and sleet, the long trek back to London.

Meanwhile, *we* have been tracking an image constructed by Esther, who is telling her story seven years after the fact, forcing us rhetorically to see and feel the anxiety, the discomfort, the desperate haste with which the child pursues her vanished mother. She has been doing this all her life; she will do it in her art and in her soul until she dies.

Finally, Esther and Inspector Bucket arrive at the cemetery where Nemo, Lady Dedlock's lover and Esther's father, is buried: "On the step at the gate," Esther tells us, "drenched in a fearful wet of such a place, which oozed and splashed down everything, I saw, with a cry of pity and horror, a woman lying—Jenny, the mother of the dead child." Esther has not yet understood about the switching of dresses. Again, she says, "I saw before me, lying on the step, the mother of the dead child." Then, when she "lifted the heavy head, put the long dank hair aside, and turned the face"—carefully paced artfulness, chilling, sensual, step-by-step delaying of disclosure by Esther the writer—she at last sees, and discloses to us, "my mother, cold and dead."

I think that Esther means neither to frighten nor to sadden us so much as she intends to batter us with art. We are shaken not by the death so much as by the life of the writing. When we read this scene, we feel great, heavy shapes falling into place: *This*, we suddenly understand, is what Esther has been leading us to over so many years, so many events, so many pages. From the buried doll self, through the buryings and exhumations along the way, to this: What Esther has, in apparent error, described as "the mother of the dead child," despite the trick of the traded dresses, is, in fact, the mother of the dead child.

The dead child is Esther. In the course of reviewing her life, she has sought—dramatically, rhetorically—to plead the case for Esther Summerson. Scarred as she is by the pox that Jo carried, she is more deeply disfigured by her early lessons in unworthiness. As ever, Dickens writes of memory; as ever, he seeks to state a long grudge or wound and then forgive or heal it; as ever, he cannot quite succeed. So his novelist, Esther, writes a rhetoric of damage, striving to forgive and to "win some love," haunting herself in the process and proving anew that an incurable wrong was done, that she wishes she were not wounded, admitting sotto voce that she still is. May we not, she wonders—or prays—love her in spite of her telling us such terrible truth?

The narrator of the third-person sections, the raging, authoritative voice that lays its charge like a lawyer and like a sapper, says of Jo's passing: "Dead, your majesty. Dead, my lords and gentlemen. Dead, Right Reverends and Wrong Reverends of every order. Dead, men and women, born with Heavenly compassion in your hearts. And dying thus around us every day." Yet this same voice gives us Mr. George, the noble soldier and heroic civilian, and Dr. Woodcourt, a man of compassion and grace, and of course John Jarndyce, selfless and cornucopian. In effect, this narrator speaks in a dialectic of alternating fury and gentleness that may remind us in its polarities of Esther as she breaks her own heart before our eyes and then declines to an all-but-simpering apology.

It is curious to read Esther's own description of the area around the graveyard when she finds her mother—"heaps of dishonoured graves . . . hemmed in by filthy houses . . . on whose walls a thick humidity broke out like a disease"—and to have to remind oneself that this is *not* the voice of the third-person narrator. Here, as two conspirators search for clues linking Nemo to Lady Dedlock, "a thick, yellow liquor defiles them, which is offensive to the touch and sight. . . . A stagnant, sickening oil . . . slowly drips, and creeps away down the bricks; here, lies in a little thick nauseous pool." I find myself easily able to confuse the two voices, the affection of each for making cruel images that evoke disgust by making inanimate objects sweat organic liquids.

Esther, at a tender moment, says of Dr. Woodcourt, whom she loves: "I saw that he was very sorry for me. I was glad to see it. I felt for my old self as the dead may feel if they ever revisit these scenes. I was glad to be tenderly remembered, to be gently pitied, not to be quite forgotten." Surely when she lists what she appreciates, she is also enumerating her goals. Yet she also,

I suggest, may simultaneously be hiding from sight by burying herself in the voice of the third-person narrator. In that voice, she can vent her large-scale fury; in her own voice, she can woo our gentle pity with a small child's complaints and with a heroism we applaud.

She often does appear as two people, scolding herself: "Now, Esther," she says, "if you do, I'll never speak to you again!" Finally, this story, in which her two aspects speak, alternately hiding and revealing themselves, is Esther's effort to achieve entirety, a novel told by one narrator in two voices. The teller is a coy Victorian woman-child, peeping at us through thickets of velvet, satin, taffeta, brocade, *and* a stern denouncer of the general sham. Esther Summerson tells England's story and her own, striving to do some good, striving to win some love if she can.

III

THE CHARACTERS IN *Our Mutual Friend*, Dickens's last complete novel, march through one another's lives, muttering to themselves about themselves, pondering their own reflections and shadows. John Harmon, assumed dead but living under several disguises, reviews his labyrinthine story in the chapter entitled "A Solo and a Duet." He tells himself what has happened and then asks himself, "This is still correct? Still correct, with the exception that I cannot possibly express it to myself without using the word I. But it was not I [who was beaten and nearly drowned]. There was no such thing as I, within my knowledge." Not a breath is taken but that its origin and effects are considered. Nothing in the world of this novel is taken for granted.

Each important character in *Our Mutual Friend* projects a self for public apprehension; they manipulate the world with

lies, disguise, sham, delusion, even body parts; they are perceived in terms of their personal fictions in this cosmos painted
by Dickens in the browns and variations of black that we associate with Rembrandt's portraits of Rembrandt grown old.
With palpable sorrow, Dickens studies darkest Dickens and the
nasty essence of the Victorian age. He organizes his characters'
experiences around mounds of garbage. He finds violence,
greed, and cruelty within his characters' warring selves and in
transactions between classes, sexes, religions, friends, and family members.

For all its public fictions about identity, the book abounds in
private fictions, too: The main characters are at one time unknown not only to one another but also to their respective
selves. John Harmon, who is also John Rokesmith and Julius
Handford, does more than disguise himself from Bella Wilfer,
the woman to whom he is to be married by arrangement; he
hides away even from himself: "there was no such thing as I,
within my knowledge." Bella is divided about her responses to
wealth, proclaiming to John Rokesmith, the impoverished secretary she has come to love without suspecting that he is the
vanished heir to whom she was as a child engaged: "that girl
[Bella herself] has often seen herself in a pitiful and poor light
since, but never in so pitiful and poor a light as now." Everyone
in this novel sees the world in light of her or his interior condition; seeing things *in terms of,* not intrinsically, these characters can only measure people or events against themselves.

They each, then, carry on arguments with themselves. Mr.
Twemlow conducts interior debates about his relationship to
those models of superficiality, the Veneerings. Bradley Headstone, the murderous schoolmaster whose violent passions are
Lawrencian, stands at a blackboard before his students and has
"half a mind to draw a line or two upon the board, and show
himself what he meant" about wishing he had attempted murder more efficiently.

Attached to the plot early on, and associated with the story's key elements—death, commerce, class, sexuality, deception—is Mr. Venus, an articulator of dead bodies and dealer in everything once living, from small animals to severed limbs. It is through his shop and through his love for Pleasant, the daughter of Rogue Riderhood, the dredger of corpses from the Thames, that we can examine the subtleties of the novel from which T. S. Eliot took the line "He do the police in different voices," intended as the title of *The Waste Land*. Like the poem, the novel is an evocation of the fragmented, tormented "accumulated scum of humanity," the "moral sewage" for whom death by drowning and baptismal rebirth is the only hope.

Into Mr. Venus's shop in a run-down district stumps Silas Wegg, vendor of street ballads, liar, and petty crook, who has been hired by Noddy Boffin, the friend of John Harmon who seems to have inherited the vast legacy Harmon was to possess. That wealth is the product of suburban dust mounds, mountains of waste matter, every scrap of which is worth money; in Victorian England, Dickens reminds us, nothing was not for sale. Mr. Wegg is hired by the illiterate Boffin to read to him. As ever with Dickens, reading is not only a way by which to rise socially but also something that permits one to "read" the world. Here, reading is a moral as well as an intellectual power, as Dickens shows when he tells of a "kind of illegibility" that steals over a man's face, masking its "old simplicity of expression" with "a certain craftiness."

Wegg, literate after a fashion, deluded and deluding and immoral in almost every fashion, limps on his wooden leg into Mr. Venus's shop to inquire, "Am I still at home?" He wonders, that is, whether Mr. Venus has yet sold his amputated leg. As are so many characters in this book, Wegg is known through his metaphoric projection: "I" means his leg, and when he talks about himself, he refers to something separate. So does Bella when she refers to the "poor and pitiful light" in which she sees herself; so does John Harmon when he describes, sub rosa, his actions to himself; so does Headstone when he prepares for murder by wearing Rogue Riderhood's clothing—he projects himself as, he *becomes*, the embodiment of the dredger. Bella sees herself in the "pitiful light" of her greed. And everyone in the novel is seen in light of—is in effect lighted, if not illuminated, by—Mr. Venus's "little dark greasy shop," which is lit only by a candle "surrounded by a muddle of objects vaguely resembling pieces of leather and dry stick." The shop's dark light is the lantern by which these characters throw their shadows.

Partially assembled skeletons stand watch; dead birds drape the counter. With pride, Mr. Venus shows off his shop to Wegg, describing "the general panoramic view":

> Tools. Bones, warious. Skulls, warious. Preserved Indian baby. African ditto. Bottled preparations, warious. Everything within reach of your hand, in good preservations. The mouldy ones a-top. What's in these hampers over them again, I don't quite remember. Say, human warious. Cats. Articulated English baby. Dogs. Ducks. Glass eyes, warious. Mummified bird. Dried cuticle, warious.

Wegg involves Mr. Venus in a plot to fleece Boffin. He makes clear to Mr. Venus that because of his confidence scheme, he now has expectations and, "under such circumstances," he does not wish "to be what I may call dispersed, a part of me here, and a part of me there." He "should wish to collect myself like a genteel person." Precisely such self-collection is the goal of each of the fragmented characters in Dickens's wasteland. That is why the shop serves as synecdoche for the novel: It is the place of dispersal for profit; it is the assembly hall of bits of death for sale.

Mr. Venus is distressed by his rejection by his beloved,

whose identity we do not learn until late in the novel. He says
of her attitude toward his profession that though "she knows
the profits of it . . . she don't appreciate the art of it, and she objects to it. . . . 'I do not wish,' she writes in her own handwriting, 'to regard myself, nor yet to be regarded, in that boney
light.' " She refers, says Mr. Venus, to "the lovely trophies of my
art." The lovelorn god of love is here an artist. His art has to do
with a secondary sort of life-giving; he rebuilds the dead; he
makes facsimiles. The living dead of the novel perform a kind
of art as they each make likenesses of themselves: See Jenny
Wren, the dolls' dressmaker, pretend to be her drunk father's
mother, and see him behave like her child; see Eugene Wrayburn pretend to be a heartless roué; see Riah, the old Jew, mas-
querade as the power in Fascination Fledgeby's money-lending
business. Mr. Venus stands for them all in their making of fiction.

But when Pleasant Riderhood rejects Mr. Venus, she is
hardly rejecting the commodification and fragmentation she
may see around her. She runs an unlicensed pawnshop; she buys
and sells the rags that these Londoners drape on the flesh with
which Mr. Venus will later deal. The "boney light" in which she
refuses to be viewed—in which she refuses to view herself—
needs further definition.

By the end of the novel, every character's projection of an alternate self is resolved. Bradley Headstone has died, clutched in
the arms of his double, Riderhood; Boffin is restored to his be-
nign ways; Harmon is loved by Bella and can disclose his identity; Fledgeby is brought to light and thus brought down; Wegg
is defeated; Eugene Wrayburn has undergone the same death
and rebirth in the Thames that has brought John Harmon back
to life, and he has married the heroic Lizzie Hexam, daughter
of another dredger of the dead.

The dark sexuality, the enslavements of class, the loss and
discovery of self—all are represented by the elements we find

in Mr. Venus's shop and in the refrain—Pleasant's unwillingness to be regarded in the "boney light" of Mr. Venus's art—that Dickens threads sparingly but suggestively through the novel. It is true that despite her childhood in the violent world of those who fished (and robbed) the bodies of dead men and women from the Thames, Pleasant has showed something of a conscience. And Mr. Venus's pride "in her own handwriting" testifies to her literacy, unusual among the children of dredgers. But it is still difficult to understand this rough-and-ready woman's objection to Mr. Venus's trade.

Very near the novel's end, Mr. Venus tells Wegg that two friends approached Pleasant on his behalf "to try if a union betwixt the lady and me could not be brought to bear." This question, presumably at Venus's urging, was posed: "whether if, after marriage, I confined myself to the articulation of men, children, and the lower animals, it might not relieve the lady's mind of her feeling respecting being—as a lady—regarded in a bony light." (Quotations in this essay refer to the Penguin Books edition [edited by Stephen Gill] of 1971, reprinted in 1985. It is based on the Chapman and Hall two-volume edition of 1865, for which Dickens read proof. The variations "boney" and "bony" are based on Dickens's decision or oversight.)

Mr. Venus, a capable and insightful man, calls Pleasant a "lady," and we must honor his vision of her, though she will never be more than a shopkeeper's wife on the lower rungs of the middle class. But he not only respects Pleasant; he desires her—"lady" or not—and we may consider that Pleasant and Mr. Venus are talking not simply about station but also about Pleasant Riderhood's sex. She does not want, as a woman, to be illuminated by the insights of a man who rebuilds dead women—perhaps what she sees as dead embodiments of herself. The premarital agreement underscores the presence—the importance—of sexuality in the minds of the characters of this flesh-conscious novel. It echoes in Pleasant's sensitivity to her

gender, her desire for privacy from prodding, fingering, articulation; it is a key to Lizzie Hexam's desperate struggle against
the manipulations and pursuits of men of the middle and upper
classes.

During the writing of *Our Mutual Friend*, Dickens conducted his affair with Ellen Ternan. It is very likely that the
conduct was, sexually, uneasy at best. And when we recall those
preserved babies floating in jars in Mr. Venus's shop, we might
consider that Ellen Ternan is thought by some to have had two
pregnancies that resulted in miscarriage or stillbirth. Mr.
Venus's shop is decorated with the same dueling frogs that decorated Dickens's study at Gad's Hill Place. And I am tempted to
think that when Mr. Venus, the artist of sorts, is rejected by his
beloved, he is an emblem for Dickens. Perhaps he is also a very
private emblem—one more mutterer to himself—of the failed
artist, the somehow-tainted lover, who brings what he sees as
life and hears it called "death."

Like so many of the neurotic, modern-feeling characters in
Our Mutual Friend, Pleasant Riderhood is uncomfortably self-
conscious. In an age of increasing invasion, her claim to privacy
and defense of her sexuality are a defense of her essential self.
She speaks to the desire of other characters in the novel to project a public aspect of themselves, according to their needs, and
at the same time to shrink from scrutiny. I wonder if Dickens,
in dealing with *his* dilemma—the public patriarch of the religion of home and hearth who had cast out his wife and taken up
with a very young actress—might not have considered his own
public self, his own hidden being. I wonder if he might not
have both appreciated and feared his own conclusions. For I
think these characters he created fear the psychoanalysis of sorts
that is his version of Mr. Venus's "art." It is the narrative articulation of truths long buried, truths surely prefigured in the
somber self-examination of David in *David Copperfield*, of
Arthur Clennam in *Little Dorrit*, of Pip in *Great Expectations*, of

Eugene Wrayburn and John Harmon in *Our Mutual Friend*. Pleasant Riderhood sees herself as *handled*. "Articulation" is a double entendre: In this novel, and in Dickens's and his characters' minds, the metaphoric projection of each of them is so powerfully offered *and perceived* that when their divided, dramatized selves are touched, each feels it on the flesh.

Ellen Ternan, evoked by but not represented as Pleasant Riderhood, at this time in Dickens's life feels Dickens on her own flesh. Determined to be a professional actress and not a cosseted mistress, she is trapped—for the sake of Dickens's reputation—in the life of the demimondaine: stashed away in houses rented under pseudonyms, subject to the lusts of a man who had been great to her and her mother and who, perhaps naked before her in several ways, now seems less than great. Claire Tomalin, in her study *The Invisible Woman*, quotes a clergyman who befriended Ellen Ternan in the years after Dickens's death. William Benham states that she told him that Dickens "had visited her two or three times a week; that she had come to feel remorse about her relations with him during his lifetime, and that her remorse had made them both miserable; and that she now 'loathed the very thought of this intimacy.' "

Our Mutual Friend is a book, a world, of reputation: You are as you are perceived. Lizzie Hexam, brave and virtuous, married at last to Eugene Wrayburn and much loved by him, is referred to at a Veneering dinner party as "a horrid female waterman." The emphasis on naming her sexuality, and the interesting confusion of genders, is a clue to the fascination (and attraction) for the upper classes in sexual relations between the castes. Although Lizzie is good, she cannot be seen that way in the world of high society—nor in the Veneering world, which pretends to height—because social metaphors are stronger than moral actualities. Pleasant Riderhood, another decent-enough woman, could also be called "a female waterman." While Lizzie's aim is domestic, Pleasant's is social: She seeks to control how she is perceived, and in what light she perceives. Behind her is Dickens's awareness of Ellen Ternan's plight, and of his own.

Mr. Venus's greasy shop, lighted by its lone candle, is a skull. It is Dickens's hollowed-out death's-head, the age's and his own memento mori. It reminds us and Dickens of mortality, the death in life that these characters' and their readers' way of living has become. And in the light reflccted from bare-bone labors, we see Charles Dickens, forlorn as Mr. Venus, collecting, preserving, rebuilding.

Pleasant Riderhood dictates the conditions of her marriage (as Ellen Ternan absolutely could not), and Mr. Venus foresees a happy ending, as Charles Dickens—for either his novel or his love affair—could not. Dickens will not refrain in his life or in his art from making fictive projections of parts of himself and those whom he loves. He will dramatize them, articulate them. In *The Mystery of Edwin Drood*, young women will be hungrily pursued, men's souls will be splintered, and disguises will be donned; the fastnesses of Rochester Cathedral, the dark complexities of Dickens's soul, will briefly be visible in that waning, bony light.

THE LANGUAGE OF STARVATION

EATING IS A political act, in fiction a political metaphor. Suicide by starvation is a vote—perhaps an act of war.

Eating is literally performed by a child in a functioning family, or by an adult who, metaphorically a child, receives bread (or the money that buys it) from the parental state or institution. Eating is a function of enablement, of somehow being fed. And eating is an act ranging from acquiescence to subservience, whether or not there is gratitude involved. It acknowledges the feeder's ability—superior power—to provide the food.

So to reject the proffered food is to reject the feeder—to proclaim to parent, institution, state that it is *not* transcendent: that its body and blood do not substantiate. Intentional starvation starves the feeder of the signs (and pleasures) of power. To starve intentionally is to repudiate and wound the world, to reverse the customary flow of psychic force by the grossest of

/ *159*

physical means: Starvation by preference is rebellion that succeeds.

Some of our supreme fictions make use of this political metaphor. Often discussed as the literature of alienation, they are rarely referred to as political. Yet Melville's "Bartleby" is as political as Thoreau's "Civil Disobedience"; Kafka's tale of family horror, *The Metamorphosis*, is as political as *The Grapes of Wrath*. Each reveals that the modern hero can triumph over the world only by dying away from it. Our literature is not only concerned with death; our heroes—those who win out over the world's thrall and terror—must die, not survive in wounded courage, to defeat our enemy—the age we have made. Survival is *not* victory. The metaphor of suicidal starvation will perhaps suggest ways of seeing how that sad vision works.

For example: the fiction of Henry David Thoreau, in which his character Henry David Thoreau, pictured as an embattled prisoner—in no danger whatsoever, and really knowing it—mocks his jailers with their "foolishness" for treating him as if he were "mere flesh and blood and bones, to be locked up." He repudiates the notion that the human spirit can be enclosed, and he says, "I was not born to be forced. I will breathe after my own fashion." That fashion presumably includes the ultimate option: not breathing at all. Although we assume that Thoreau was not suicidal, we cannot assume that his literary persona was unaware of his power, through death, over life. For he says, "If a plant cannot live according to its nature, it dies; and so a man." It is a threat of refusal to be wrongly nourished by a wrong world.

One reason for the appeal of "Civil Disobedience" to present-day readers is the modernity of Thoreau's imprisonment. It is not so important that he thinks himself important for defying the state. And it is not important, even, that he thwarts the state until he is bailed out. What matters, and what is so modern, is that Thoreau, who should be a victim, decides the quality and degree of his victimhood: He insists on the primacy of the self. *He* decides that it is his jailers who are captives, not he; *he* decides that a work of art about his victimization is a weapon against diminution; and *he* decides that a man in prison may die by the most dramatic and metaphoric way, if he chooses. The victim, then, controls his response to the state's control. He is no longer a nineteenth-century hero who watches himself be disposed of. He makes an artwork of self-disposition as he preaches "Disobedience to Civil Government" and loyalty to self-government. No wonder Gandhi saw the essay as a weapon deadly to empire.

Gandhi's phrase "passive resistance," which does not occur in "Civil Disobedience," does occur in Melville's "Bartleby the Scrivener: A Story of Wall Street." The story, published in 1853, four years after Thoreau gave his lecture, is of course read as a metaphoric tale of alienation. We need only recall the architecture of the nameless narrator's law chambers to verify such a reading: The chambers are on Wall Street, walled off by surrounding high buildings; half opens on a view of darkness, half on light; the two clerks, Turkey and Nippers, are complementary halves, one a fury of passions and inefficiency in the morning, the other in the afternoon; the lawyer's room is walled off from theirs; inside his room, a screen separates him from Bartleby; behind the screen, Bartleby stares through a window in a "dead-wall revery" at a wall of bricks. Clearly, the story is concerned with separated parts of the self, with being walled away from one's realest self, and from the world.

But it is also a story of political subversion and starvation. Paid to work for a bastion of the establishment, a man "not unemployed in my profession by the late John Jacob Astor," Bartleby subverts the workings of the law firm, drives the lawyer from his own offices and into "fugitive" wanderings about New York—and perhaps into recognition of his own humanity—by saying, "I prefer not to." By forcing society to hear a preference, instead of witnessing mere refusal, Bartleby forces it to acknowledge a statement of taste and judgment—hence the fact of the whole human being behind the statement. Esthetics here become political weaponry.

Bartleby then reinforces his succession of preferences not to—his suggestion not only that he *is* because he refuses but that not-being is preferable to that world which is—by starving to death. By refusing meals that the lawyer bribes a warder to give him, Bartleby rejects the world ("I am unused to dinner"), denies its ability to nourish him, and removes its power to do so. By facing his prison wall (forcing the lawyer to feel shut away—the jailer jailed) Bartleby, echoing Thoreau's proud rhetoric, establishes by his death that he is robbing the state of its power. He makes the biggest protest, states the clearest preference, compels the world to acknowledge who he is and what he wants by forcing its representatives to dig a hole and place him in it. And he makes a metaphoric prison of the world that survives him.

For Kafka, all the world is a prison, and it is not certain whether he makes his family a paradigm for that world, or the world a model for his family. Part of his greatness, probably, is that the two are so interchangeable: He is an artist of the very narrow and the huge at once. The body of his work is a study of power and powerlessness, and here is how he describes family love, in his *Diaries* for November 12, 1914: "Parents who expect gratitude from their children (there are even some who insist on it) are like usurers who gladly risk their capital if only they receive interest." Emotional nourishment is extortion, and this is Kafka's revolution against it:

> The parents and their grown children, a son and a daughter, were seated at table Sunday noon. The mother had just stood up and was dipping the ladle into the round-bellied tureen to serve the soup, when

suddenly the whole table lifted up, the tablecloth fluttered, the hands lying on the table slid off, the soup with its tumbling bacon balls spilled into the father's lap.

That entry in the 1914 *Diaries* shows how much Kafka saw eating—the family communion—as political, and how much he wanted the tables turned in his family, which he loved and which dominated him and which he feared. It is how he saw the world.

The same family group appears in *The Metamorphosis*. Trapped in his room, Gregor Samsa rebels and locks his family and employers out. He is the world's victim, and he denies his body to its appetites by changing so utterly that he no longer satisfies the hungers he once did. He is abandoned (freed) by family and employers. The metamorphosis, effected by his buried rages, removes him so far from the world that his own appetites can no longer tolerate that world. He starves away from it, repudiates it, and achieves his emancipation; he is now called "the thing next door," is freed even from invocation by name.

At the beginning of the novella, immediately after his transformation, "He could almost have laughed with joy" at the sight of bread and milk. Eventually, he puts food in his mouth when he happens to pass it: He "kept it there for an hour at a time and usually spat it out again." At the end, Kafka merges spiritual and physical with his evocations of food: "Was he an animal, that music had such an effect on him? He felt as if the way were opening before him to the unknown nourishment he craved." Although Kafka uses the language of eating, his character speaks of music, not food. He has already made "the decision that he must disappear," and he is beyond corporeal nutrition. The language reinforces what the rejection of food has already told us: that Gregor votes against the world by leaving it.

In "A Hunger Artist," of course, the focus of the story is starvation itself. While it is a parable of the artist and his needs, it is also an enactment of the artist's political desire—to force the parental world to respond to him, perhaps even love him: The hunger artist says, "I always wanted you to admire my fasting." Kafka goes beyond Melville in creating political protest and in analyzing it; the artist here is helpless, the revolutionary feeble, before his own compulsions (Dostoyevsky would agree), and he is *forced* to protest. Unlike Bartleby, who prefers to starve, the hunger artist says, "I couldn't find the food I liked." Kafka's politics here are interior as well as exterior, and the outsider is, within himself, his own meek victim; if it had been possible, he would have surrendered to the world: "I should have made no fuss and stuffed myself like you or anyone else."

In the metaphorical terms I have used, politics enlightens art, art politics. Saroyan's romantic hero of "The Daring Young Man on the Flying Trapeze" (1934) seeks to do both. First, he speaks directly to political matters:

> It was good to be poor, and the Communists— but it was dreadful to be hungry! What appetites they had, how fond they were of food! Empty stomachs. He remembered how greatly he needed food. Every meal was bread and coffee and cigarettes, and now he had no more bread. . . .
>
> If the truth were known, he was half starved, and yet there was still no end of books he ought to read before he died.

This young writer seems to speak of the political so as to point up its separateness from the artistic truth at which Saroyan (and his protagonist) aims: that it is good to die for art, that out of such death comes that state ("dreamless, unalive, perfect") that a mind chained to its body cannot achieve. Perfect art, and the perfect rewards of the artist—"It made him very angry to think that there was no respect for men who wrote"—are available only when human imperfections are removed: in death. Yet this young man is highly political; he and Kafka's hunger artist are, in fact, quite similar. They are coercing the world to love them by dying away from its nourishment; they are reversing the customary design of power. They are both forced by what is outside their control—the one by economics, the other by absence of provender his body can tolerate—to starve. Yet each is, clearly, fully satisfied only by his death; his dying tells him that his death is what he has wanted, is the only means by which he will achieve what he desires. As Saroyan's writer says, "His life was a private life. He did not wish to destroy this fact. Any other alternative would be better." Of course, the grave's that fine and private place; there are no alternatives.

Knut Hamsun, in *Hunger* (1890), is interested in showing us that his protagonist will starve rather than not write. But he does not want to die. He wants to live *in order to write*. He is inordinately healthy, listening to his interior self, following its demands that he live the life of the writer. But when, as Robert Bly points out in the introduction to his 1967 translation, the interior self tells him to work and live, at the risk of no longer writing, he does so: "The cakes disappeared one after the other. It didn't seem to matter how many I got down. I remained ferociously hungry. Why didn't they help!" Even if this is not the nourishment he should have if the world were perfect, he will eat in order to live in the imperfect world, in which artists do not triumph. His subconscious, which has directed his course throughout the novel, tells him that he ought to survive. So he does: He remains in the world and is fed by it, accepts its power over him—"So he gave me a job to do. . . ."—and provides a symbolic opposition to the examples of Kafka's hunger artist and Saroyan's daring young man. Hamsun's writer, perhaps like his author, is a political survivor, an artist who fails; Kafka's and

Saroyan's artists, who succeed, cannot survive. Have we, in truth, come so far from the apotheosis of Chatterton? Did the poetry of Plath, Berryman, and Sexton threaten us, with their deaths, because we loved them insufficiently? Were we—the world, the blank wall at which they stared—to be punished by their leaving us? And is that part of the reason for our disproportionate celebration of even their most minor work?

Saroyan uses hunger to make us feel sorry for his protagonist. The weakness of the sentimentality in Saroyan's fiction, particularly in "The Daring Young Man on the Flying Trapeze," is that Saroyan will do anything to make the reader love his characters. He will demean them, kill them, break their hearts—and not always because the character's inner necessities require such torture; they suffer in order that Saroyan achieve our response. So the young writer starves himself, or enjoys his starvation, because Saroyan believes that the strategy will draw the reader in. Indeed, there is the other motive—to show how the artist flies out beyond mere physicality. But we might want to note that the tactics of literary starvation include a playing on the most sensational, least rational, qualities of the reader.

So Dickens, in *The Old Curiosity Shop*, has Little Nell starving on her journey through the Midlands not only because an industrialized society, and a virulent Quilp, are heartless toward her—although these are part of Dickens's strategy of starvation. His most important motive, one suspects, is to make us feel sorry for Nell: to pull us into his world, and, at his mercy, on his terms. Starvation can become a political act on the writer's part, then. He starves his character to assert maximum power over the reader's emotions. We become incapable of rejecting him. He feeds us—*his* idea of nourishment—against our will.

An extension of this idea is the way some writers kill their characters off by violence in order to place us at their mercy. If we disregard the lesser book-club novels, and look at someone like Forster, the point is clearer. Character after character is killed in *The Longest Journey*, and not necessarily because he is doomed by his fate. He dies so that Forster can force his characters to react. Before he knows what to do with Ricky—kill him off, of course—he knocks people down like dominoes, hoping that the deaths will force his characters into focus with what lives remain. While employing the tenderness of the body count, Foster nevertheless insists on a realistic fiction. His Salisbury Plain writhes with life, while his characters are corpses, killed so that his ideas may live. Compare these gratuitous deaths with the coldly rendered, metaphorically functional deaths in *To the Lighthouse*. There it is clear that the novel is about the absence of Mrs. Ramsay, about time: The deaths that an artistic sensibility will try to undo must therefore occur. The reader is not only shocked by the deaths in the Ramsay family; he is saddened. And as Lily Briscoe tries to reverse time, recreate life through her vision, the reader mourns her failure. Mr. Ramsay springs up from his boat as Gregor Samsa's sister springs to her feet (the butterfly metamorphosing from the pupa that Gregor really was). And because of the deaths, one feels that something basic has been at stake.

Arthur Clennam, in the Marshalsea at the end of *Little Dorrit*, defeated sexually and societally, decides to die; he loses his appetite and his sense of taste, begins to starve and sicken. When Dorritt returns, she lures him back to the world. She reads to him in a voice that evokes Nature's ("At no Mother's knee but hers had he ever dwelt in his youth") and in her voice "are memories of an old feeling of such things": She becomes his mother, the prison cell her womb; he is reborn to the world. Steinbeck effects such a rescue at the end of *The Grapes of Wrath*. Starving, having decided to die—"He said he et, or he wasn't hungry . . ."—the old man is saved by Rose of Sharon. He sups from her nipple, is metaphorically her child. Both are examples of Caritas Romana, that classical image of charity celebrated in Renaissance, neoclassical, and Romantic art, as the wife, daughter, or mother suckling a man who is starving to death in prison. While the sexual implications of the image are immense, one can be equally struck by the fact that the image is so frequently political: the man as child is nearly always in jail, a victim of the state.

Roman Charity, a rebellion by brave woman, is political in that the will of the state is defeated. But what if it is the will of that state that we survive, suckle at the breast of government? In that case, the breast, whether proffered by a government or by an Earth Mother, becomes antagonistic to the self-government of the citizen who wishes to exercise his ultimate will by dying. The modern protagonist slaps the breast aside.*

But Kafka says that he cannot. In Kafka, everything is lost. Even his hunger artist loses the satisfaction of intentionally starving away from the world. Kafka insists on denying to man any franchise whatever: Life is what happens to us, not what we do. So even the officer of "In the Penal Colony," who is in charge of the apparatus that engraves onto the prisoner's body with needles and acid the commandment—BE JUST!—that the prisoner is said to have violated, himself becomes a victim of the machine. He elects to leave, in the fashion he chooses, a world he sees as unjust, but he is denied the right. The machine disobeys him: "This was no exquisite torture such as the officer desired, this was plain murder."

"In the Penal Colony" is a political story that contains elements we have found to be central to the modern terror state. Like "Bartleby," Kafka's story has a figure disenfranchised by political change; instead of (as in the Melville) loss of a

*I am indebted to the fascinating discussion by Robert Rosenblum in his "Caritas Romana After 1760: Some Romantic Lactations," in *Woman as Sex Object, Art News Annual* 38, eds. Thomas B. Hess and Linda Nochlin (New York: Newsweek, Inc., 1972), 43–63.

Chancery post, or of a job in the Dead Letter Office, we have in the officer a middle-management figure, a My Lai murderer who obeys orders. But there is a new commandant, and the political climate of the penal island has changed. Instead of dedication to the apparatus of tutelary torture, the officer sees a web of intrigue: the new commandant is influenced by gross sexuality (his laughing ladies) and he is unenthusiastic about the formerly honored torture ritual. The opposition between the old commandant and the new, and the importance of the palimpsest of plans for torture, and the prophecy that the buried old commandant will "rise again and lead his adherents," are all suggestive of an Old Testament world opposed to a New, or anyway an old God seen in opposition to prevailing faith in a new one. If that is so, Kafka politicizes even the heavens.

The point, whether the story is cosmic or earthbound in its implications, is that the dutiful officer is an Eichmann figure for contemporary readers—not merely because he obeys the old commandant's orders with such zeal, no matter their perverted justice and morality, but because his primary concern is *to keep his job*. Like so many middle-management types, the officer's central allegiance is less to the beloved old commandant than to the machine of torture and its tending: "I can no longer reckon on any further extension of the method, it takes all my energy to maintain it as it is." One recalls Gregor's fear that he will lose the job he hates—or Kafka's same worry.

The job is to process victims for the sake of the process itself. The victims, of course, receive no justice as they are tortured to "BE JUST!" They are paradigms of the terror state's victims (and of humankind in the terrifying cosmos in which such states thrive). It is important, then, that they be fed. The officer explains the apparatus:

Here, into this electrically heated basin at the head of the bed, some warm rice pap is poured, from

which the man, if he feels like it, can take as much as
his tongue can lap. Not one of them ever misses the
chance. I can remember none, and my experience is
extensive. Only about the sixth hour does the man
lose all desire to eat. I usually kneel down here at
that moment and observe what happens. The man
rarely swallows his last mouthful, he only rolls it
around his mouth and spits it out into the pit.

The officer's happy description is that of the man who knows
and loves the intricacy of his work. It is not difficult (though it
is awful) to imagine Mengele explaining that they are sorted
here, the sick are lined up here, their clothes are dropped off
here, and here is where I stand to watch them.

"Not one of them ever misses the chance," says Kafka's officer: The breast is not pawed aside, and the world forces itself
down the throats of the condemned. The sixth hour is gener-
ally the moment just before death for the prisoner. He does
not rebel when he spits the food out; he is considered enlight-
ened (and ready for burial). He goes to his death with a mouth
encrusted by what the world would feed him. Self-
determination dies with him.

It is that kind of death in life, inflicted by others, that Beckett's Molloy fights off. When Lousse requires of Molloy that he
live with her, and forces food upon him—"the substances she
insinuated thus into my various systems"—she makes him her
replacement for the dog she says he's killed. He is punished by
feeding, reduced, as Thoreau says he is, in "Civil Disobedience," by the minions of the state who "had resolved to punish
my body; just as boys, if they cannot come at some person
against whom they have a spite, will abuse his dog." Thoreau in
jail looks out "through an iron grating which strained the light."
Molloy, in Lousse's imprisoning house, looks out through a
window on a moon strained by its bars so that "two bars divided

it in three segments, of which the middle remained constant, while little by little the right gained what the left lost." Each writer makes the moon—one of the world's facts—a function of his imagination. So, too, does he make the imprisoning world itself and its attempts to nourish him with its facts against his will functions of his imagination. And through the imagination each escapes, by refusal, or, in Thoreau's case, postulation of refusal, of what the world would serve for dinner.

Young women do so daily by retreating into the psychic agonies of anorexia nervosa: They find that they cannot eat; they vomit up their food, are skeletons, sometimes die. The women who withdraw their appetites look sexless, finally, like the wide-eyed young Kafka—whose photographs put one in mind of staring, emaciated concentration-camp survivors.

A woman who retreats is Gail Godwin's protagonist in "A Sorrowful Woman." *"Once upon a time there was a wife and mother one too many times,"* the story begins, and by the end she is sealed away in a housekeeper's room, unable to cope (and unwilling to cope) with husband or son. She becomes "a young queen, a virgin in a tower," and her rebellion is analogous to Gregor Samsa's, and to Bartleby's, as well; in her room stocked with cigarettes, books, bread, and cheese, she "didn't need much." She eventually prepares to die by baking bread, roasting a turkey and a ham, making three pies, custards; she does two weeks' laundry, makes drawings for her son, writes love sonnets to her husband. In other words, she performs all the chores—symbolic actions, as well—the world (according to Godwin) expects of a wife and mother. Another reading, of course, is that she does so not out of love, or guilt, but that she leaves behind mementos of what killed her. Her metaphorical suicide message, then, is one of harsh accusation: *Look what your expectations have done to me.* The husband discovers her corpse and simultaneously the son asks, "Can we eat the turkey for supper?" She is their meat. She refuses to be nourished in their world; it is they who devour her. She partially resembles Kafka's hunger artist, and her family—the world—are like the young panther in the dead artist's cage: "the joy of life streamed with such ardent passion from his throat that for the onlookers it was not easy to stand the shock of it. . . ." But they "did not want ever to move away."

Such withdrawals are often central to recent fiction by women, for the women in these works are, foremost, victims. There is a premium on female victimization, and publishers, riding the commercial crest, see to it that we have an over-abundance. Although the focus is new, though not so new as the press agents and book reviewers tell us, we need think only of Prufrock, Leopold Bloom, Lady Brett, or Caddy Compson to remember that all of our significant modern protagonists are somehow imprisoned. And we need think only of Eudora Welty's Jack Renfro and Julia Mortimer to remember that our fiction is not without heroic figures.

But we recall our heroes infrequently. For each Rosacoke or Milo Mustian, Artur Sammler, Invisible Man, we can—and do—name a hundred protagonists who are destroyed by the world. The likes of Lowry's Geoffrey Firmin have given the hero a bad name: We call him dead. He isn't, but he must, it seems, die to triumph in contemporary writing.

For when our heroes do succeed, it is in the dark heart. We see them in the agonies of a defeat and epiphany that we tend to accept as metaphoric of our own self-consuming enlightenments. They win by living *within*. Their emblem is the maggot of hope that writhes in the age's excrement.

Examining the hero in terms of the world—the pressure of too many frightened people, the force of institutional events, the daily diminution—we turn back to Kafka, who says that one may not refuse by means of muscle, courage, the imagination. His hunger artist *must* starve; the officer's dying prisoners have to lap at the teat they're strapped to. According to Kafka, that we insist on accepting the world's nourishment, no matter how much we desire to forsake it, is the tragedy of our entrapment. It is the reason such wise political parabolists as Gandhi, Sakharov, Dick Gregory, Cesar Chavez, or the protesters in Long Kesh prison have insisted on showing us that they starve on our behalf. They are sometimes, now, these starvers, a prick to our conscience. When they die, we may call them heroes. And so it is with our literary heroes. They do not win on our behalf unless they achieve mortality. When we write our most prayerful art, the hero, in opposition to his nineteenth-century predecessor, survives. When we write this age's interior realism, the hero survives only metaphorically, by choosing to die in his skin, rather than with thousands in a furnace, or a mass grave.

TERRENCE DES PRES

TERRENCE DES PRES haunts me, and his presence arrives each time with startling power. When I see his dust-jacket photograph—his eyes are brave and frightened at once, his face is made of shadows; he is both sinking and swimming—I am physically jolted. He came to the Chenango Valley of upstate New York, where Colgate is, from rural Missouri by way of Eliot House at Harvard. He brought with him the blessings of the Trillings, a doctorate about Romantic poetry, real expertise in fishing, a huge project on the witness borne by Holocaust survivors, a divorce that grieved him, pain and guilt about Jay (the son he missed so terribly), and a determination to write about the workings of language in his culture with such mastery that he would be as important to literature as Lionel Trilling, say, or Matthew Arnold. I know a woman who changed his work and whose writing was changed by him. I know a man who hates his memory and who rejoiced about his death. A writer in my department was confirmed in the direction of his poetry because of Terrence. I know a colleague of ours who thinks of him tearfully every day. I knew students who took his course in the literature of the Holocaust and whose lives were permanently altered. He was a devastatingly attractive man, and I knew students who risked (or nourished) their youth on affairs with him. I knew the wives of faculty who risked their marriages with him. My mother, having met him once, telephoned to vamp him. A professor I know, hearing that Terrence was to marry Elizabeth Hecht, went berserk, I'd have to call it, and was considered, for a while, a physical threat to Terrence and herself. His soul was haunted. What good writer's is not? I know that he was married to a brilliant woman he dearly loved. She had helped him to control his use of alcohol and to achieve health. She made him smile like a boy. It was a smile that lit up the night one often saw in his face.

He wrote as if his life were at stake. Never mind the fame he wanted and achieved, and never mind the money he might have made or the undergraduates who held him in awe. Many of us, readers and writers, experienced enough to understand the human amalgam were also impressed and even awed. His work on the Holocaust remains important. So do his essays on contemporary poetry and the relationship of art to politics. Something of what he needed to find and needed to say is in the conclusion of his essay on the poetry of Thomas McGrath: "Against the old ultimatum, not thunder and the fall of sky, but the street's careless laughter and the sigh of a neighbor next door." He was an engaged man who wanted to believe in Whitman's wished America, and he died too young.

Terrence Des Pres and I were drawn to each other, in the 1970s, because of our commitment to writing. We sustained each other in the loneliness and doubt of our work. Terrence was a lapsed Catholic; he wrote about murdered Jews; he knew how to catch a fish and cook it; he was able to see at once, and usefully explain, how I habitually mismanaged the openings of the stories I was writing. I, a very secular Jew, was immersed in writing fiction inside the domestic music—wife and sons, dog, garden, the interior *doing* that means life—that Terrence wanted; I could never fish nor hunt; and I had read, and could speak with him about, some of the bearings of witness of which he was writing. In college departments, one finds resolute non-writers, men and women who disappoint themselves, and those who hired or who tenured them, with their determination not to produce the written work that was their youthful promise. They often grow sour, they flourish in campus politics and by way of classroom mannerism, and they dislike busy writers. Terrence and I rubbed such men and women wrong, and we bolstered each other when they made clear that we had gone against their grain.

He took strong prescription medicine for an injured, very painful back. He drank a lot. Sometimes at the end of a night, especially as his work on the Holocaust grew more harrowing—as the large eyes in his handsome but sometimes masklike (though sometimes passionately animated, sweetly smiling) face grew haunted—he became loud in his sad declamations. His voice grew high, and he breathlessly claimed about the awful documents he had to ponder, and about his efforts to write commentary that was worthy of the survivors' pain. He would speak of guilt and of the bravery and beauty he discovered in accounts of unspeakable suffering. He would talk, as writers often do, with a simultaneousness that nonwriters find difficult, about his moral purpose and his ambition for fame. He spoke so quickly, he grew breathless. His eyes seemed to widen, to darken. I recall this happening one night as he began to roll and, with his elegant fingers, flick empty glasses on the kitchen table. They came as close to the edge as he was. He struck them harder, and then shoved, and then finally threw them, one after the other, until they flew and shattered, and the tabletop was clear, and Terrence was in tears.

Early on another evening, I heard brakes screech in our driveway. It was Terrence in his shabby car. As I watched from a window, he ran in a hunched, wounded way to our door. White, panicked, a hand at his chest, he said that he was having a heart attack. I tugged him into my car or his—I can't remember which—and drove him to the hospital, fifteen miles away. On the examination table in the emergency room, as a doctor questioned him, Terrence, suddenly calm, his voice soft, said, "I'm writing a book about survivors of the Nazi camps." The doctor waited for what he would think of as *real* information. Terrence gave a long, accurate summary of his work. His color was good, his breathing normal, his eyes clear. And no one there had doubts about what had been squeezing his chest. He had found what most writers searched for, consciously or otherwise, all their working lives: the subject that was metaphor for the interior strife that drove them to be writers. He had also found some of the danger in work that is, to its maker, a matter of life and death.

We were friends when *The Survivor* was published to great applause in 1976. I brought him three copies of that week's *New York Times Book Review*, on the front page of which Alfred Kazin celebrated the author and the work. Terrence had opened champagne. Although there were quibbles from other reviewers—about his not having studied documents in their original language, about the integration of E. O. Wilson's work into his closing chapter—there mostly were not. His fame grew; speaking engagements proliferated. And he became, I felt, a trader on his celebrity; he began, I thought, to trivialize the subject on which he had written so powerfully. I said that, in certain newspaper articles he wrote, he was demagogic. He said I was jealous of his sudden importance. We became less than friends. After the 1979 publication of my novel *Rounds*, in which Terrence claimed to find himself represented as less than heroic, we stopped knowing each other. Years later, after his marriage to Liz, our mutual friend the novelist Leslie Epstein, whose *King of the Jews* we each admired and about which each of us had written, in 1983 or 1984, sought to draw us together. We spoke again with pleasure. We exchanged work. We were en route, I think, to being friends, wary and worried or not, once more. We might have come to trust each other again. Judy and I at last dined with him and Liz at his invitation, and we had agreed to dine together soon again. Not long afterward, I flew off to a reading, in November of 1987, and on my return was greeted at the door by Judy with her news of Terrence's accidental death.

A year later, I was reading on an airplane. The book was the one Primo Levi completed before his suicide in 1987, *The Drowned and the Saved*. It is Levi's least forgiving and possibly most brilliant book. Its essays have the power to make a man in the darkness of a night-flight airplane gasp and draw inquiring looks. On the back endpaper of the book I find in my handwriting—I remember writing it in the amber cone thrown by my reading light—"Pp. 39–41: Tension between this and TDP's findings?" I wanted—I *needed*—to ask Terrence what he thought about Levi's words. For while Terrence had written in *The Survivor* about "the need *to* help" being "as basic as the need *for* help," and that "in the concentration camps a major form of behavior was gift-giving," Primo Levi said that a newcomer "was derided and subjected to cruel pranks, as happens in all communities with 'conscripts' and 'rookies,' as well as in the initiation ceremonies of primitive peoples: and there is no doubt that life in the Lager involved a regression, leading back precisely to primitive behavior."

I had always thought that Terrence's work had much to do with his own need to survive the failure of his first marriage and the pain he accused himself of having caused. I thought he needed to try himself and finally to reach the verdict, having weighed the sorrows and spiritual decline he associated with his divorce, that he still might be a good man. His work in general and the particular passage I've cited—there are dozens like it—suggest that what he needed to conclude in his life he sought to find in the lives of strangers in other kinds of hell. Levi, that remarkably sensitive, hopeful, but utterly honest, wounded man, seems to have known otherwise. Although he, too, cited some instances of decency in the camps, he wrote, "It is naive, absurd, and historically false to believe that an infernal system such as National Socialism sanctifies its victims: on the contrary, it degrades them, it makes them resemble itself. . . ."

What I needed to do, in that airplane that night, was talk to Terrence. I wanted to know what he thought. I almost *felt* the discussion in advance, and I hungered for it. The realization that I could never have it struck me with sudden power, and I remember that I reached up to extinguish the light and I wept. I finally mourned.

Some of his friends from later years, who knew him after I did, have spoken about Terrence's stepmother, and the vicious, loveless circumstances in which she forced him to live his young life. They have suggested that he was an inmate in his life and that he came to see in the lives and deaths of inmates of the camps a metaphor for his youth. When we were friends, he didn't speak about his childhood in those terms. I don't know people who were his friends then to whom he did. He rarely mentioned his stepmother. He spoke of poverty, and his mother's crushing death when he was very young, and his father's career as an itinerant schoolmaster. He spoke of times when he saw to the domestic chores of the house, the feeding and clothing of his siblings. I believe that he could not speak *to himself* in the seventies about the oppression he suffered as a child—that came later, most especially, I think, with Liz's help. But what he felt and spoke of in the seventies was guilt. At this time of his life, the metaphor that seemed to him to fit was that of victimizer to his former wife and child; it was only later, when he had confidence and encouragement enough, that he might have seen himself as victim. There is much in that deep interior priority to admire.

I put a Count Basie album on our stereo set one evening and, as Basie vamped, I made playing motions with my hands to accompany his spare prelude to some Kansas City blues. Terrence asked with delight if I played. I told him that I didn't but that if I could, I would give up my teaching to play blues piano in a roadhouse. He told me that he'd earned money playing in a bar and that he had hoped we could—his words—"have a jam session."

His face was young with pleasure when he talked about making music, and it relaxed, too, when he spoke of his father's movement from school to school, even though those moves were harrowing. Each move meant a new house to rebuild or build from scratch. It meant a journey into childhood frights for Terrence and the other children. The images he spoke remained with me. I used them when I wrote a novel called *Take This Man*, which was published in 1981, and which I imagine he didn't read. In it, writing about someone absolutely other than Terrence, I employed those images he had shaped with such pleasure. It is possible, especially in light of what he later told friends about his childhood, that these were some of his happiest times. Surely, in them he and his father find a nonverbal way to love or woo or anyway make emotional contact with each other anyway, and they worked at *making*. The construction of a world figures in almost everything that Terrence wrote.

I wanted to save those moments, and I wanted to save them not only for myself. I gave them to him while we were not friends, because once we had been. I served myself, and I made *my* fictive world, and I did on his behalf, too, the work that writers do: save feelings, instants, and visions from being eaten by time.

Here is one memory of my novel's character, taken from Terrence's words:

> His father had taught in a school like this; they had driven for days to get to it, they had built another house for themselves, and his father had gone every day to teach in the high granite-and-brick building— make-believe miniature castle, probably built from discarded blueprints for a runt armory—with hard yellow light from classroom windows glowing on the parking lot and playground.

Later, the same character recalls "This wasn't anyplace to do with what he'd called home, where he'd been born to circulate in hot counties with a lonely schoolmaster who often was mother, father, architect, and carpenter for them." And then this:

> He tried to place himself . . . anyplace without his father and the motion—new classrooms, the faces looking up as he walked in to one more first day; orange lumber, bought cheap because undried, warping in the sun as they worked; roofs on which they rode in spite of his hourly mistakes; his father's dimpled flanks as they showered from a rain barrel after building a porch; his confidence, each time, despite his father's growing reservations, that this was what

his life was supposed to be—and he couldn't see . . .
how he might come one day to live another way.
That frightful blankness, blank as the dark his father
carried him through in the pitching truck, must be
the bright future his father sometimes mentioned—
the life that was different from this. . . .

But he missed him, as if loss were sudden and
new. No matter what that man had done and been,
he had been the man who straddled the roof and
laughed. He had been the one who carried them
through the nights and strange landscapes, and who
had made them, finally, homes. It had been that
man's hand at the back of the boy's thin neck, in
whatever nameless countryside.

One night in 1975, I called for him at Olmstead House,
where he lived. His quarters were on the upper floor of a Colonial home he rented from the college; he lived in a couple of
rooms, kept a mattress on the floor for a bed, and was surrounded by thousands of books and records, which I thought of
as his furniture. On his wall was the smiling photo of his beautiful and very young mother. He was in another room, I in the
living room, and as I waited, I looked at his books. Opera was
playing on the stereo. It was always at that time either opera or
Janis Joplin, whose hoarse, edgy voice reminded him, he said,
of his edgy boyhood. I saw an open notebook beside the chair
in which Terrence had been sitting. I had to look. He was
smarter than I, and I would learn something, and my work was
as a magpie of lives. Here is what he had written: "Stories, first
of all, store time." What I wrote in *Take This Man*, out of Terrence's memories, is the usual battle with loss; but maybe for
Terrence and me, despite the distance between us at the time of
writing, it was the jam session we had wished for.

When I remember Terrence, as I do so often, I think about the willingness alloyed with an almost insisted-on casualness with which he took our son Ben, who was about eight, on little fishing trips. Fishing meant a great deal more to him than he told Ben, with whom he was gentle and tutorial about technique, but otherwise silent, Ben said. In one of his finest essays, a memoir that begins in the third person before shifting to the first, and which is shaped like a short story, Terrence remembers his Missouri boyhood. He writes about fishing—about a boy, he discloses after three pages, who was "of course . . . myself, a self more vital, compact, *pure* [my italics], like wood within the inmost ring of a tree whose life has reached to many rings." He writes, "Amid the damage of living I find purchase in that uncluttered coming to selfhood of a boy. . . ." His work was about what must not be forgotten; and perhaps his own greatest loss was that participation in "the blessing of boyhood." He wrote in search of innocence, hoping—insisting—that he would find it again, even in modern life's worst horror. He never wrote again—at least for publication—about fishing: "rites that for a million years kept men living and in touch with awe."

The grace he saw as lost did goad him. He felt that it could be rediscovered amid the damage of living. He required of himself that he search for decency in humankind's sewage. And all the while, some of what nagged at him was the boy he had been, the self he saw as dead. I think that much of his work was an attempt to save that boy, to find him—in the worst we can do to others and ourselves—alive and blessed and pure.

But he doubted as much as he wished to believe. Despite his search—his prayer—for what was good, he also wrote, "Except in memory, a grace that is lost stays lost." His salvation would be his memory, then, his saving from time what otherwise was vanished. His innocence would be in what he wrote. He would search, but he might not find, I think he suspected. In writing of John Gardner's life and death, he referred to "childhood notions of guilt and the cross, a boy's desperate wish to be good and be loved."

He was both.

EVEN THE SMALLEST POSITION

As unemployed Americans of our time cry for jobs, good books out of print cry for republication. Some are louder than others. Some of the unemployed we notice more because of their dignity and our sense—it grows as we consider them—that our own transactions are diminished without their participation.

Such a book is Leslie Epstein's *The Steinway Quintet: Plus Four*, which was allowed to go out of print before most of us knew it existed.*

*While I wrote this essay, Leslie Epstein wrote two more novellas about the hero of "The Steinway Quintet." The three stories were published as *Goldkorn Tales* (1985) and they were monumentally misperceived and misrepresented in The *New York Times Book Review*. He published an immense comedic novel, *Pinto and Sons*, about a nineteenth-century Jewish medical student in the American West who lives with the Modocs; his reviewers were not up to the task. In 1997, he published his long-awaited *Pandaemonium*, which takes

We are lessened by its absence from the marketplace. I invite your attention here to bodies that float like blimps, the Angel of Death on the Lower East Side of Manhattan, the murder of the Jews of Europe, and the making of music in Vienna by Gustav Mahler. For all this, at once, is the stuff of the title story of Mr. Epstein's book.

"The Steinway Quintet," like all good stories, is about what we have and don't want, what we want and don't have, and what we don't want to know we do and don't have. Since the story is an advertisement for a job, I dedicate my essay on this unjustly ignored work to the politicians—in publishing, in Washington, and in the classroom—who help to make *job* rhyme with *Job*, and to whom out-of-print books are leftover goods.

After being rejected by *The New Yorker* and *Esquire*, "The Steinway Quintet" was initially published in 1976 by *Antaeus*. Following its appearance there, the story was selected for *Best American Short Stories of 1977* and became the title story of a book published by Little, Brown. But the print run was only fifteen hundred books (of which, the author thinks, half were sold) and every book was mistakenly bound without the last page; extant copies contain a tipped-in final page in a typeface different from that of the rest of the text. By the end of 1977 or early in 1978, the publishers remaindered the book (that is, sold off the unsold copies), and it has since been unavailable. The author's literary agent had arranged for Epstein to receive fifty copies, which were boxed and left in a corridor for pickup by the mail service. The janitorial service picked them up instead, and they floated that night, with exhausted facial tissues and unwanted

---

its place beside West's *The Day of the Locust* as a great novel about America focused through the lens of Hollywood, and the reviewers got it right. He is writing new tales of Goldkorn. And in fall, 1998, the Living Writers course at Colgate University, in partnership with Southern Methodist University Press, republishes *Goldkorn Tales*. Leib lives.

correspondence, as incinerator smoke above the skyline of Manhattan. It is not always easy, as so many people are learning these days, to be of use to the world.

Yet nothing Epstein writes is inconsequential. He is able to offer humor and cataclysm—at once; lyric and epic concerns—at once; your individual heart and all of my Europe or America—at once; cold, precise description of the blood's hot rush—at once. From his first novel, *P. D. Kimerakov*, through *The Steinway Quintet* and *King of the Jews* (which I would suggest to be a major novel for our time) to *Regina*, and his recent novels, Epstein has been ample and brave. Who else has dared to write funny lines about the Holocaust? And he's a master of that peculiar form, not a novel and not a short story (*"Don't call them novellas!"* cried Katherine Anne Porter, who wrote them so well): the long story. "The Steinway Quintet" is a splendid example of that form's richness.

Listen to its opening lines: "Good evening, my name is L. Goldkorn and my specialty is woodwind instruments, the oboe, the clarinet, the bassoon, and the flute." The narration is Goldkorn; the story is a voice. As a musician, Goldkorn tells you his name and his instrument in one sentence: He is what he plays; his job is who he is; Goldkorn is his work. Note, too, that he is speaking directly to you about his essence. Be warned: You are responsible for intimate news, and he is vulnerable and charming. He not only wants you to know something; he wants you to *do* something, to feel something, maybe to yield something up. Great fiction shows us all fiction, in certain ways. Goldkorn is a voice of fiction, and he knows you are there. He has politely addressed you. Like his clarinet or flute, his story is an instrument. Goldkorn—like all the narrators on wonderful pages who have pulled the reader up close enough to smell the warmth of their skin—is after results.

Listen, now, to the early paragraphs of the story:

Good evening, my name is L. Goldkorn and my specialty is woodwind instruments, the oboe, the clarinet, the bassoon, and the flute. However, in 1963, on Amsterdam Avenue, my flute was stolen from me by a person I had not seen before, nor do I now own any other instrument of the woodwind classification. This is the reason I play at the Steinway Restaurant the piano, and not clarinet, on which I am still proficient, or flute, with which my career began at the Orchester der Wiener Staatsoper. Examples of my work on the latter instrument may be found on recordings of the NBC Orchestra, A. Toscanini conducting, especially the last movement of the Mendelssohn-Bartholdy Fourth Symphony, in which exists, for the flute, a wonderful solo passage.

I wish to say that I am an American citizen since 1943. My wife is living, too. These days she spends most of her time in bed, or on the sofa, watching the television; it is rare that her health allows her to walk down the four flights of stairs that it takes to the street. In our lives we have not been blessed with children. Although the flute was in a case, and the case was securely under my arm, a black man took it from me and at once ran away. It was a gift to me from the combined faculty of the Akademie für Musik und Darstellende Kunst, when I was fourteen. Only a boy.

See how his days and health as well as his wife (whom he does love) come second; first comes his art. For this is a story about art and artists in an age of enormities. It is not a reflexive, metafictional story told by itself about its writing or its author; there is subject matter and a high regard for—a long and crafty gaze upon—the world of people just as dopey and spectacular as you and I. But it is also about the art on which Gold-korn does, or tries to, thrive.

As he makes his history and his domestic life, his work and love and much of his plight, known to us in a very few lines—they are not mere information, the sort of brand-name stuff that second-rate writers think of as convincing details—we realize that how Goldkorn gives the data tells us who he is. As he tells us his past, he returns to the violence—street crime in this case—that surrounds his life (and yours) as it informs his exposition. But remember the tender "Only a boy" that occurs at the end of his reminiscent second paragraph: It is the lyric note sustained in the story, the soft-petaled flower that lives where street dogs trot.

The story begins, and we are in the Steinway Restaurant on New York City's Lower East Side. The musicians, waiters, and customers—nearly all of European Jewish extraction—are playing or listening to minor music. But the players take their work and themselves seriously, for they are musicians and, like Goldkorn, they live their art. Listen, as he describes the restaurant's atmosphere, to Leib Goldkorn creating silence with sound:

> Salpeter picked up his bow. Murmelstein, also a violinist, put his instrument under his chin. Also present were Tartakower, a flautist, and the old 'cellist, A. Baer. For an instant there was silence. I mean not only from the Steinway Quintet, which had not yet started to play, but from the restaurant occupants, who ceased conversation, who stopped chewing food; silence also from Margolies, Mosk, Ellenbogen, still as statues, with napkins over their arms. You could not see in or out of the panes of the window, because the warmth had created a mist. Around each chandelier was a circle of electrical light. Outside,

on Rivington Street, on Allen Street, wet tires of cars made a sound: *shhh!* Salpeter dipped one shoulder forward and drew his bow over the strings.

It is, for an instant, the cultured and elegant Old World. The story's epigraph is from Shakespeare's *The Tempest*, also about magic and art, which is set on an island, away from the world, the better to make the magic happen and the better to make us accept it. The restaurant is such an island, too—"You could not see in or out . . . on Allen Street, wet tires of cars made a sound: *shhh!*" Even rude intrusions of the coarse world become the audience at a concert as it hushes itself—*shhh!*

Goldkorn and the others live within the magic (or needs, or zaniness: what you will) of their vision. They see *their* way. So when two men walk in, they are described (erroneously, we soon learn) as "a tall Sephardic Jew and a short Jew, also of Iberian background." They are seen as such because the see-ers receive the world in their terms, terms of "mister Sigmund Romberg's *The Student Prince*," "roast duck and Roumanian cracklings," and, naturally, glasses of hot tea. Even when the two tough guys make their move, the watchers see that "both Sephardim were holding big guns." Deaf Mr. Baer, unaware, keeps playing the cello. One of the toughs breaks his bow, demanding (and achieving) silence. Baer remonstrates. The tough jumps on the cello and shatters it.

A protest is raised: " 'I am an American citizen since nineteen forty-three' some person cried. The voice was familiar. It was certainly that of Leib Goldkorn." Thus, he inserts himself more directly into the historical parts of his narration, but in such a way—such a marvelous way—that he is his character while he is his narrator, as he addresses us months after these events took place. After the naïve exclamations and further savageries (when the cook is pistol-whipped, the musician Goldkorn asks us, "Is this not in many ways an act as terrible as the destruction of a violoncello?"), only *then* does someone say, "Friends, these two are not Jews." At last they realize that two Puerto Ricans swallowing amphetamines are holding up the restaurant. The world has invaded their littler world of small magic, their eccentric vision. And much of the rest of the story will demonstrate the contest between what practical people tell us the world really is and the spell under which Goldkorn and his companions wish—probably need—to live.

At this point, Goldkorn breaks off—there is a chapter break on the printed page. He returns with:

> Greetings! L. Goldkorn once again. I have paused for some time. It was necessary to mix medicaments for my wife. Now she is sleeping, my life's companion, with no obstruction of nasal passages. Sweetly. Also, it is sometimes desirable to settle the nerves. I am too old to speak of such terrible things, the destruction of property, attacks to the head, without becoming myself upset. This is to explain the presence of Yugoslavian schnapps. Alcohol is good for you; it allows to breathe the hundreds of veins which surround the heart.

This will be the structure of the telling—his present plight seen in the context of his history. We will read in two times at once. We will experience storytelling as a necessary journey to the past—necessary for Goldkorn to take, necessary for him to force or lure us into taking. And we will see that he stalls by breaking off; he temporizes because while he wants to be in his past, for whatever needs and practical purposes, he also does *not*, periodically, want to be there himself. He does not wish to face the actualities of the invasion of his dreamy life by the Hispanic holdup men. He has learned that invasion's lesson and he shies from recalling the truth of cruelty in the world.

Ishmael, telling us *Moby-Dick*, did the same. *Moby-Dick* is a recollection and performance by a survivor. Like Coleridge's Ancient Mariner and Pip in Dickens's *Great Expectations*, the narrator of "The Steinway Quintet" is also a survivor, condemned to wander restlessly and to tell his urgent tale. Goldkorn evades the telling at least momentarily, as does Ishmael. Goldkorn runs to his wife or his schnapps. Ishmael flees to long diversions about whaling. But as the whaling chapters become increasingly metaphoric, mirroring Ishmael's apocalyptic concerns, so Goldkorn's evasions are also futile. He must return to the tale. And we see another truth about storytelling: Just as the artist seeks to persuade us, often against our will, and for his own ends, so he must labor against his own will. Narrative history in sentences may be a sentence that the storyteller serves. The tellers may even be said to serve a function by serving such communal sentences on our behalf. Perhaps that is their job. They will require payment from us.

As Goldkorn now recounts the life of V. V. Stutchkoff, the Steinway's owner, we hear again the common story of the life of much transplanted European Jewry, including the story's first reference to the obvious—the Nazi murder of the Jews. The point is important, for as we see Goldkorn's present life and past adventure simultaneously, each informing the other, we will also see the Holocaust informing events at the Steinway.

Stutchkoff, hearing the commotion of the holdup, slowly— he is tremendously fat—hauls his great weight upstairs to the dining room from his office. "It seemed as if there would be no end of him," Goldkorn prophetically says, describing how the huge form deliberately rose and rose into sight. Frightened, amazed, finally threatened, the bandits fire away as Stutchkoff, like a magic being, ascends. They kill him, plunder the register, and try to make their escape, but the back door is locked, and they cannot flee through the front door because Stutchkoff's great corpse is blocking it. Police sirens approach.

Now that the world has invaded the magical island of these marvelous characters' collective imagination—Epstein is so like Chekhov in rendering collective states of mind—the curtains close over again. We are once more away, on the island of *The Tempest*, in the province of Leib Goldkorn's vision. One character rages about sewing on a yellow star, and we remember the Holocaust, and why these people see aspects of their lives in certain inescapable ways. Stutchkoff's wife kneels to untie her husband's shoes and necktie—it is a duty of the Orthodox Jew—so that the soul may fly up. At once, there is a differing opinion: Someone suggests that she does her duty so that the Angel of Death will not be tempted to linger. (Meanwhile, a diner, who has introduced himself as a Freudian analyst, declares, "She is undoing the knots that might hinder the release of . . . his *anima*. It's Jungian psychology." Epstein's wry humor glows with life, in the presence of death, as a profession is put on its guard, a state of mind satirized, and a character drawn— all in three sentences.)

There is, of course, rabbinical debate among the Jews. To live, among them, is to endlessly discuss. Margolies offers Zev Wulf of Zbaragh as his authority on responses to the Angel of Death. Ellenbogen counters by citing the Maggid of Mezritch. The widow ripostes with the Spola Grandfather:

"No, Shmelke of Nikolsburg! The dead man must not see his own spirit depart!"

"Mister Ellenbogen, am I not correct in assuming that the purpose of this action is to prevent the Angel of Death from becoming entrapped in the glass?" [They are covering a mirror.]

"That is a valid interpretation, Mister Margolies."

"Pfui!"

Doctor Fuchs spoke from the viewpoint of science: "I agree with the negative opinion of our friend

Mister Mosk. These are Jungian daydreams. A regression to primitive thinking. Even children—"

"Look, gentlemen! She has finished!" It was Salpeter, our first violinist, who was speaking. "Now dear V. V. Stutchkoff, patron of the arts, may depart!" Every person's eyes swung back to the corpse.

"THIS IS THE POLICE DEPARTMENT SPEAKING. YOU ARE SURROUNDED. COME OUT WITH YOUR HANDS IN THE AIR. YOU MUST SURRENDER."

That voice came from an amplified horn. One of the gangsters, an adolescent, a boy, shouted back: "We ain't going nowhere! We got hostages! We're cold killers! You gonna find out, because we going to kill them one by one!" He threw a blue-colored pill into his mouth. His colleague smiled, and swallowed a red one.

"Mama!" The cry came from the rear. "Mama!" Martinez, the cook, raised his bloody head from the floor.

Again Leib falters, and the story breaks. He evades what he knows, but then he is forced—as artists must perform, as lovers must woo—to return:

Hello? Hello? Leib Goldkorn here. What a poor memory! Have I mentioned my performance of the *Italienische Symphonie?* Or have I not? Only a short time ago I happened to hear this same recording on radio station WQXR. The difficult aspect of playing in the orchestra of A. Toscanini—of course there were also many joys—was tempi, tempi, always the tempi! An artist went as fast as he could and—"No, no, no, no: Allegro! Allegro *vivace!*" The key to the final movement, this thrilling passage, is breath control:

whether I possessed it or whether I lacked it you will judge for yourself.

Now the radio is off; this is because of the television for the entertainment of my wife. She is watching from the sofa, with her medicaments on the table. A red cotton nightdress and a white cap: adorable, the little mouse! You will pardon me? I am sipping hot milk with hot coffee. No sugars. I am fond of sugars. However, Clara has diabetes. I think now we are having a spring morning. The tree on the street has birds in it and the buds of leaves. The clouds are not serious clouds. I have suffered since February from a disturbance in sleeping. A result of the events in the Steinway Restaurant? A sign of advancing age? Brandy from plums is good for this condition. Yes, but the bottle is nearly empty. An inch at the bottom is all that remains.

Notice how Goldkorn's thoughts insist upon running together, as in the second sentence of the story and, again, in the paragraphs I've just quoted. He experiences a great deal simultaneously; his life, hard as it was, cannot be easy now. His style tells us this. He is his voice, and in small ways he reveals—probably because he wants to—that he is afire within.

Now: The heat is turned off, the restaurant is embattled, the crooks are frightened and high on pills, and soon they are full of liquor. They are holding rich Jews captive, they think:

"Oh, sure, you wanna have a little drink!" the youth opened the *fine champagne* and filled to the brim a tall highball glass. "So, Mister Weinberg, Steinberg, Feinberg! You wanna drink to one hundred thousand dollars?"

"Ha! Ha! Ha! Weinstein, Feinstein, Steinstein!

Ha! Ha! Ha!" The tall man, the man with the successful moustache, slapped the face of his younger colleague. "Names of Jews!"

"Ha! Ha! Listen, Mister Greenberg—"

"Mister Goldberg!"

"Ha, ha! Drink it down!"

Only once before in my life, thirty-two years in the past, have I tasted a liquor of this class. The Hispano-Americans continued to slap one another. They each swallowed a pill. They put more of the cognac into my glass.

"My name is L. Goldkorn, specialist in—"

"Ha! Ha! Ha! We gonna get a hundred thousand American dollars!"

The temperature falls, and so does the snow, and the night passes. Goldkorn recalls—his vision controls him, remember—the snow having blown from right to left (like Hebrew writing). "Then that night, in some respects no different from any other, came to an end," he remembers. He reminds us of the Passover seder question: Why is this night different from any other night? The seder commemorates the passing of the Angel of Death beyond the doors of the Jews in the Captivity. Their lives are somehow informed by captivity. And their funny debates on responses to corpses and the Angel of Death might suddenly strike one as more than funny, though never, in Epstein's story, as less.

The police send Spanish-speaking negotiators to lure the crooks out. To resist, they command the Steinway Quintet to drown out the police by playing. It is a savage scene. The quintet plays the "CanCan" while Baer, in shock, moves his arms, as if to play, but with nothing held within them. And then the quintet plays the "Barcarolle" while the tall thug, Jesus, considers the rape of the woman who, at the story's beginning, had requested "Some Enchanted Evening." The story is about enchantments—naïve ones, artistic ones, drugged and criminal ones, and even enchantments with America. The rape is about to begin. Goldkorn thinks:

> *Here the poorest boy may rise to the highest position in* *the nation. Many have done so: many more will do so in* *the years to come.* From what source, and from what distant time, had this thought come to my mind? At once I knew. These were the words of Judge Solomon Gitlitz, spoken to me, as they have been spoken to thousands of others, upon the occasion of my American naturalization. I stopped playing Offenbach then. I stood up on my feet. Murmelstein, nearby, pulled my clothing:
> "Don't make trouble. Sit. Sit down."

But the enchanted, innocent immigrant from Europe's latter hells says, "Listen, young man, you must not do this. You have a fine tenor voice." And we must laugh, or decide not to cry. Goldkorn goes on: "What were the possibilities of such a situation? I tapped the shoulder of her attacker, who slowly turned toward me his head: 'You are dragging the flag of your country in the dust.' " The rape is beginning:

> I heard gasping. Behind my back Jesus had risen on all fours. The foot of the woman had lost a shoe. It was at this point not possible to look longer. "Young man, one thing more. My dream . . . was to ride on a tramcar. These went through the streets of Vienna, throwing out sparks, and each was equipped with a musical bell. If you work hard, if you learn to speak American English, you will be able to ride in a silver airship. I guarantee this to you! We have a land of

opportunity! Do not commit this terrible crime. Stop
your colleague! It is nearly too late!"

"Oh! Oh! Oh!"

The second shoe of the lady was gone. Each of
her legs was now forced into the air. What happened
next was that Leib Goldkorn, I myself, had knocked
the hat of the tall Puerto Rican off his head onto the
floor. Not only that; violently I was pulling his hair.
Success! The man rolled aside, and the lady—she
was missing her collar of pearls—began to adjust her
purple dress.

The rapist and his partner are outraged. And we hear the
old, the familiar, refrain. "The Jew is going to die." And:
"Going to die: All Jew." So we learn a lesson about the courage
of this artist and about heroes—remember that Leib Goldkorn
tried to forestall Jesus, at first, by telling him stories about his,
Goldkorn's, life: He is always the tale-teller—and we learn that
the world colludes, strangely enough, in creating the enchantment we thought to be exclusive to the people of the Steinway
Restaurant. The world speaks in the voice of these people's history—"Going to die! All Jew."—and Goldkorn (and we) are
learning a hated lesson. In the context of the story, Goldkorn is
the enchanted party; we, the readers, his audience, are of the
world. So we listen, now, not only because we are learning
about Leib Goldkorn; we are, reluctantly, learning about—and
perhaps also denying—what might be aspects of the world, and
therefore of *us*. We are not Goldkorn the narrator. We are the
ear in which he whispers. Yet, might we not wish to become like
silly Leib, who acted so bravely? Especially if it means that we
aren't a party to what the world threatens him with? The story
makes it difficult for us to be neutral, no matter how alien these
enchanted Jews might be to our lives. Can a story make us Jews,
and artists, and victims of a frightening world? V. V. Stutchkoff's

corpse begins to answer these questions by turning "warm and somewhat maroon" while a patron, a Jew, as if in Europe in the thirties, protests that he isn't a Jew, but a Greek, and begs to leave. (He reinforces his Greekness by crying out in what he takes to be Greek: "Bazouki!" he will cry. "Metaxa!") The corpse's bulk before the door keeps him from it. And Goldkorn once more, on the page of his story, turns away.

When he returns, he is drunker, more disturbed by his present life and his memories of the past. He says, "Of the events of three months ago I shall speak no longer. Why should I continue? What more do you want to know? There are not any surprises. How could there be surprises when I am here, alive, a survivor, speaking to you. The suspense element is gone." Like every artist who performs, Goldkorn knows his audience in advance and feels forced to emulate them, in self-defense, by speaking as his harshest critic. Perhaps representing Epstein's worries during composition, but surely Goldkorn's own, Leib bemoans the fact that the crucial life-and-death note, the cornerstone of suspense—Will Our Hero Survive?—is sacrificed by the convention of first-person narration that only the living address us. But the complaint also tells us that more than breathing is at stake here. How breathing—quite literally *breathing*—is accomplished, as we shall see, is one of the story's crucial concerns. So, Goldkorn whines, he can't continue. So you dutifully beg him to go on—as he wanted you to. Please, you say, it *isn't* boring, I'm enthralled. And, having heard what each artist craves, he relents. Like the voice in Beckett's *The Unnamable*, "in the silence you don't know, you must go on, I can't go on, I'll go on." He does. And so does the enchanted lunar world of the Steinway Restaurant:

> "All things get worse," remarked once Sigmund Freud, who lived at Berggasse 19, only a few blocks from my boyhood home; "they don't get better." Of

course the famous alienist was referring to the condition of living persons, but at the Steinway Restaurant, on Wednesday afternoon, it applied to dead
people, too. By this I mean the corpse of Vivian
Stutchkoff, which now unmistakably smelled. It was
not hot in the room, although it had grown uncomfortably warm. The problem was the airlessness. Not
a fresh breath came to us from the world outside.
The smoke of Tartakower's, and others', cigarettes
hung in layers over our heads. And with every in-
halation, even when done through the mouth, came
the smell of—it is difficult to put the experience of
one sense into the language of another: it was a thick,
sweet smell, and a tangy smell, too. Like boots,
partly, and partly like caraway seeds.

"He stinks!" said Mosk, the Lithuanian waiter.
"P U!"

Also, he was for some reason swelling. Large already, an impressive man, Stutchkoff had begun to
bulge even further—not dramatically, not all at once,
but steadily, like bread that is rising. By two o'clock
his buttons were straining, and several had burst. But
perhaps the most painful of these transformations
was the way in which his skin altered its color. It had
been, that morning, pink and rosy as if through some
miracle he had been frozen alive. Think of the pain
for Hildegard Stutchkoff, seated nearby at the window, as that complexion deepened to purple and then
turned an absinthe green.

And the analogy to the European Jews' experience also continues—they were criticized for not resisting the Nazis, perhaps
with stiff dead babies in their arms instead of guns. Murmel-

stein, crazy with fear, begs the corpse of the legendary boss to help him. One of the bandits calls:

> "No talking! Talking not allowed! This is dead individuals! Talking to ghost? Ghost? Ha-ha-ha! No such thing! Ain't spirits! Jew! Listen! Ain't anything! Ain't anything! Ain't anything!" With the gun in his hand, Jesus was striking Murmelstein, a parent, on the back of his head.
> "Hey, cut it out!"
> "You are striking a trained musician!"
> "No! No blows on the head!"
> The staff of the Steinway Restaurant had become agitated. Someone restrained the hoodlum's arm. Someone else—this is true, I am an eyewitness—began to strike him upon the hip. Let people say what they wish; let them even deny it. We acted, friends! At that hour we fought them back!

At this point—note how much shorter the intervals have become—Leib, his stamina failing, breaks for psychic cover once again. He returns to speak more directly about his wife:

> Clara is not well, after all. I thought it was the croup but she is making a sound as though she meant to bring up her phlegm. There is also incontinence of the bowels. We treat this as a little joke between us, but if I dared, if it were not undistinguished, I would request that she wear rubber pants. Am I not speaking of a disgraceful human condition? What a scandal! And what is the point? Tell me! She does not even know that she is alive! "Am I living or dying?" she said. A better way to treat old people would be to

kill them. Kill them off would be better! There is no
mind in her. No mind left! . . . Already it is growing
quite dark. But where was I? Yes, I remember. I
would accept any employment in the woodwind area,
if necessary even the saxophone. In the percussion
group I have at times played the piano. Is that something you already know?

And now he has revealed his primary purpose—he is asking
for work, for what was once called "a place." He seeks a place
as an artist, and probably in other terms, too; he is a man
displaced in life by life itself. While the "Help Wanted"
columns of newspapers advertise available jobs, I, when I
was unemployed, and millions of Americans unemployed at
this moment, and probably Leib Goldkorn, too, would claim
that the advertisements of we who seek a place would properly be labeled "Help Wanted." Leib calls upon us for this
help.

In a long, beautifully understated scene, the Steinway Quintet turns on the spotlight, assembles near the piano, and plays
Viennese music in honor of Stutchkoff. They respond to the
general dark, and to their light, and to themselves. Leib plays
Tartakower's flute. Listen:

As our program continued, this feeling of close-
ness—better to say an absence of division, of divi-
siveness—grew to include those with whom I was
playing: Murmelstein, Tartakower, A. Baer, Salpeter.
It was as if the Steinway Quintet were a single person, giving a solo performance, as if invisible threads
bound us one to another, so that when Salpeter
moved his arm upward I felt myself pulled ever so
slightly in his direction. And at last there grew to be
a similar bond with those who were listening below.

We could at that time hardly see them—only the shine from a pair of eyeglasses, a white shirt collar, the napkin on Margolies' arm. Like heads bobbing in an ocean of darkness. Then I felt myself to be not this Leib Goldkorn, no longer the separate citizen, but also a part of that ocean, like a grain of salt, no different from those other grains, Mosk, or Ellenbogen, or the woman, Hildegard Stutchkoff, or the lifeless corpse of her husband, yes, even—do not be alarmed by what I now say—even the two murderers, for they were a part of that ocean, too. That ocean. That darkness, friends. We know what it is, do we not?

The music bridges the ocean as Prospero's magic reaches over the ocean to and from *The Tempest*'s enchanted island. Leib Goldkorn is not alone as, perhaps, for instance, now and then, the storyteller is not alone when he is doing his job.

There are many curses in this story—that of brutality and hatred and bigotry; that of the losses to the erosions of time; and that of *self.* The curse of self, as Goldkorn shows us, is the artist's curse. See how pleased and even surprised he is by the connectedness he feels, if only for a moment. We, of course, begin a conversation with Leib Goldkorn at this instant, if we haven't done so before, by telling him that we are also drowning in self; we know what he means; we envy his connectedness; we want to feel it, too. And suddenly, for the space of, say, a quarter note, Leslie Epstein connects us—non-Jewish, perhaps, perhaps not habitual appreciators of art, much less artists; perhaps sensing that we would not choose to spend much time with this schnappsy, hand-waving, sentence-drifting, dandruffy, and liver-spotted man who, with his language, lures and then dodges us, drops and grunts to pick up once more his story's thread. Epstein connects us to this foreign person as nimbly as

Ravel's *Bolero* once seduced the boys and girls of more classically innocent days. This, too, on Leslie Epstein's part, is an act of enchantment.

But the world of the camps is still with us. As at the camps, the captors strip the captives of their clothes, and the people at the Steinway hear, "Get your clothes off! Yids, move your asses!" Leib Goldkorn describes the victims in a familiar way: "All of us, musicians, waiters, patrons, were huddled together, as if on the lip of some common grave. Our bodies in the light of so many bulbs were extremely white. Ghosts of ourselves when clothed."

It is time for magic. The legendary rescuer, former patron, and present corpse, V. V. Stutchkoff, stirs:

> From the open mouth of the restaurateur there now issued a thin gray-colored shadow, a mist, a kind of a cloud—impossible to know what precisely to call it. Steam perhaps. Perhaps smoke. Everyone saw it slowly rising, more and more of it, growing taller, spreading outward, almost the size of a person.
>
> "Ghost!" Chino exclaimed, although in a whisper.
>
> *"Un diablo!"*

Leslie Epstein's magic recurs: he remains *funny*. Ellenbogen, naked except for his socks and citing the Maggid of Mezritch, turns all the Steinway's chairs upside down, so the corpse's soul won't be tempted to have a seat and stay awhile.

The strange mist rises, descends on all within, then rises again, and all are magically weeping. It is tear gas, of course, thrown in by the police. The floor begins to shake and strange lights descend from the sky. "Angel of Death," the crooks scream. Naked, but with the hidden key to the back door, the captives escape. Leib Goldkorn has fled us and returned, on his narrative's pages, once more. And the magic of the Steinway Restaurant goes on while Leib anxiously waits for the doctor, whom he has summoned to his wife. As in the story's past the captives flee, this happens:

> What we saw was that between us and the Stein-way Restaurant the snow was actually rising. It was a whirlwind. At the top of this swirling storm, a black shape hung in the air. It neither rose nor descended, but simply remained, roaring, in defiance of gravity, of physics, of reason itself. From the belly of this form columns of light shot downward and played over the surfaces of the snow.

Looking back, Salpeter points toward the door of the Steinway:

> This had swung open. Standing inside it was Vivian Stutchkoff. He appeared to be stuck. He backed up, onto the light of the chandeliers, then came forward and once again caught in the doorframe. It was at this point, naturally, that my own sanity came into question. . . .
> . . . On the third attempt, by turning a few degrees sideways, Stutchkoff got through the door. He came then bobbing toward us. Our party retreated to the opposite curb. "Golem!" some person cried. Margolies and Ellenbogen were rocking in prayer. Still Stutchkoff came, enormous in size, rising and falling, skimming the snow, like a gas-filled balloon. I barked with laughter again. . . .
> . . . Stutchkoff, meanwhile, had glided to the center of Rivington Street. There he paused, bouncing about, turning left and right; then he fell face down

into the snow. A tall and a short Puerto Rican stood
in his place. It had been some kind of trick! Yes! The
restaurateur had been their shield!

Laws of science and facts made clear seem to explain such
miracles as these. We, of course, want to know why and how
such events can occur. But I think that we're disappointed as
much as we're relieved by unenchanted explanations. We often
want to believe in magic. We are, when we read, children
opening the *Arabian Nights*, and we want the spell to go on,
even if it means letting enough of the grown-up world in, dis-
guised as data, gas, the use of a corpse as a shield, if *that* is
what it takes for Sheherazade to keep talking. This is what
fiction rises to; it disproves the finality of death (the body
walks through the door), and yet it rubs our noses in death's
total truth. It is magical and it is mundane, simultaneously. (I
should remind you that Charles Dickens, in *Bleak House*, has
a man explode in a greasy, tallow-smelling puff because of
spontaneous combustion caused by the ingestion of a lifetime's
overdose of cheap gin. Dickens was so hurt when critics
pointed to the scene as an unscientific flaw in his majestic
novel that he came to believe in his own magic. Rather than
revise the scene's impossibility, he came to love it—it is the
usual author's cheap trick. When *Bleak House* was reprinted, he
staked his reputation, in a preface, on there *of course* being
such a phenomenon as spontaneous combustion; *lots* of people
explode because of gin, leaving their bedrooms empty except
for some grease on the wall and a strange smell, as of under-
done mutton. As I have said: In great writing, we find all great
writing.)

Goldkorn flees his history, and us, one last time. He returns
to bring us up-to-date on dead musicians, jailed malefactors, his
dying wife. He gives his address and tells us, "I would appreciate knowing of even the smallest position, on any type of mu-

sical instrument." The reader is addressed directly: He has the power of a god. As we think of what has unfolded, and then think of the events in our own physical and psychic lives that we are powerless to control, we might realize how we, the gods hearing Goldkorn's prayer, are as powerless as mortals. Affirming such a frightening realization through such a subtly constructed metaphor— it turns one's notions of a god upside down—is no small achievement in a story.

Goldkorn is powerless in every conventional sense. He is desperate for money and is, obviously, out of work. He cannot pay for schnapps or for the doctor. He can never replace the flute, stolen from him in a barbarous world. He admits to drinking too much, and to being insufficiently religious in any Orthodox sense. But art, as we know, is magical. So Goldkorn *does* have powers. Art may imitate time, as Goldkorn has done, in his comings and goings, to give us an illusion of hours passing. Art can also shatter time, as Goldkorn has done, by giving us past and present at once. Art can *keep* time, as in the playing of the music of, say, Sigmund Romberg, by old European Jews on the Lower East Side. And art can invent time, as Goldkorn does in returning to his own childhood, and to the time of innocence in the life of civilization—before it, like Leib, fell upon hard times.

"Yet," he says—and it's humankind's ultimate reply to the outer dark—

> Yet I am speaking truthfully when I tell you I feel myself to be now the same person who received the gift of a Rudall & Rose many years in the past; and like that young boy I am still filled with amazement that merely by blowing upon such an instrument, and moving one's fingers, a trained person may produce such melodious, such lyrical sounds. You are no doubt aware that with the flute the breath passes over

the opening, and not into a mouthpiece, as with other woodwinds. Its music is, therefore, the sound of breathing, of life. It is the most ancient of instruments, and the most basic, too. A boy can make one with a knife and a hollow twig. This is what shepherds did, playing to sheep.

In one of contemporary literature's most life-affirming passages, Leslie Epstein turns a musician's story into music itself. Here, we have biblical and Greek lyric; we have a domestic story of a couple in poverty and sore plight on Manhattan's West Side; we have the story of the camps and the Russian tales and plays of group dilemma. The voice of the story is similar to the voice of prayer nearly anywhere driving home insistently the need of the storyteller to *say*. All of this is present in "The Steinway Quintet": unmistakably a wonderfully authentic, idiosyncratic, and individual work of art.

Goldkorn's voice is his story, and he ends his appearance before us in the guise of a two-thousand-year-old gust of breath. It is the breath of life, then, that begs the world for work. Music and the song of language, in the air or on the page—*life itself*—is looking for a job.

THE UNSCRUPULOUS PURITY OF GRAHAM GREENE

I was returning without much hope to a country of
fear and frustration, and yet every familiar feature as
the *Medea* drew in gave me a kind of happiness. . . .
A stone Columbus watched us coming in—it was
there Martha and I used to rendezvous at night until
the curfew closed us in separate prisons. . . . I wondered whether in the last month . . . she had chosen
a different rendezvous, and I wondered with whom.
That she had found a substitute I had no doubt. No
one banks on fidelity nowadays.

IN THIS EARLY passage from his 1966 novel of Haiti, *The Comedians*, Graham Greene gives us his trademarks: the journey
into fear that brings a kind of happiness; a love affair that is il-

licit; a relationship requiring faith but which is faithless and impermanent; imprisonment.

In love, Greene has taught us, we are spies. We serve a beloved, and often (we may think) unselfishly; but we also always serve ourselves. We ferret smells, the temperature of skin, the glottal click of a fragment of whispered word. We seek the knowledge, sensual or otherwise, that will let us covet—*protect*, we claim; *possess*, Greene suggests—the beloved. Whether we love or claim to love a woman or man or nation or god, we are also, always, loving ourselves. In honesty, we worry whom we love more. To love, Greene says, is to doubt.

Ours has been called the Age of Enormities, and if we start making lists—Shall we cite the Holocaust? The Gulag? The A-bomb? Rwanda? The ethnic cleansing of what was Yugoslavia?—then where shall we begin? How, ever, will we end? One response to the vastnesses of love, especially in the Enormous Age, is this century's syllable: *doubt*. We, who have survived this far, should consider in the light of the century soon to shut down what at its beginnings were considered probabilities: a God who cares; a social order fundamentally good; the growth of nations where safety and even advancement are available to those who seek it; an end to tribalism. He was born in the century's young days—1904, Berkhamsted, in England's Hertfordshire—and he began to have his doubts quite early on. Publishing from 1929, he ended his final compilation of fiction, *The Last Word and Other Stories* (1991), with this last locution: "self-hatred." Proclaimer and denier, contemplator and adventurer, reviewer and explorer, lover and husband and religionist and writer and negator of the vows one makes in every one of those activities, Greene was, as he called his early novel, *The Man Within*. He was never of one mind. He was the dark region he ventured forth to explore; he was the regime to which he'd sworn fealty; he was the spy who betrayed it. In whatever setting, and in whatever tone, his subject finally was doubt.

He was a literary artist who was never betrayed by his prose. It is clean, unmannered, inimitable. Product in part of his early journalism, in part of his desire to be read by as many readers as possible, in part because he hated lies—faked language turns septic—Greene's spare, plain writing is singular. In a contest that awarded first prize to the best imitator of Graham Greene, his pseudonymous entry came in third; his subtleties eluded the judges, who took for granted the cool gray-yellow light his writing throws on the distant, hellish countries, and some not-so-distant arenas of moral struggle, in which he specialized: places in Africa and Asia, in Central America, and Geneva, the London suburbs, the soul.

Greene's prose reminds me of his dismaying, bleached-out pale blue stare, so familiar from dust-jacket photographs and descriptions. He regards us with it in two evasive autobiographies, four children's books, two biographies, five collections of essays, four books about travel to hot and scary places, four volumes of stories, and twenty-four novels. We have, then, fifty-four places in which he might be thought to offer aspects of himself for our inspection. But finally he has stayed hidden.

He is heard from in movies, through Michael Caine and Richard Gere in an adaptation of *The Honorary Consul*, Richard Burton in *The Comedians*, Alec Guinness in *Our Man in Havana*, Alan Ladd in *This Gun for Hire*. He enjoyed films, wrote for them, wrote wonderfully about them, relished their possibility, described the cowardice and stupidity of most of them, and was as attracted as the rest of us to their meretriciousness. He wrote *The Third Man*, which starred Joseph Cotton and Orson Welles, and its harsh realism as well as its yearning toward sentimentality—Greene's ending, in the story he wrote before he wrote the script, shows the hero landing the woman who in the film eludes him—suggest to what extent Greene shared the follies and weaknesses of most of his readers.

Follies were his subject matter, finally—how, in love, we

betray the beloved; how, worshiping God, or a god, or a hope of one, we betray that hope or wish; how, striving to do good, we cause damage.

A convert to Roman Catholicism in 1926, he betrayed the woman for whose love he converted. A lifelong Catholic, he denied that he was a Catholic writer, described himself as a Catholic atheist, and wrote again and again about worshipers called to their God but driven also to treachery. Attractive to women and eager to love, he wrote about lovers whose needs ultimately caused them to harm irreparably those they adored. Widely regarded in his native land and the literary world at large as a great writer, he was to the end denied recognition by the Nobel committee. Rumors attributed his exclusion to anti-Catholic sentiments among some on the committee, and to his expatriate—his un-English political—life. He died in Provence after living there for years with a far younger woman—a fate a number of writers in my acquaintance would settle for. About the literary politicians who decried him, we might use Greene's own words about Ford Madox Ford: He died, Greene said, "with the kind of enemies a man ought to have. . . ."

Greene wrote thrillers which early on he called "entertainments," to distinguish them from his more serious work. By the time he published the profoundly moving espionage novel and love story *The Human Factor* (1978), he had stopped making that distinction. He was right to do so. For whether he was writing about an alcoholic priest who sought to evade his Lord, or about a correspondent who foresaw, in the fifties, America's future in Vietnam, or about an assassin on the loose in England, he was incorporating action and reflection, religious doubt and political betrayal, and, always, the quiet agonies of failed love.

He made sexuality into struggle, worship into a kind of murder, and self-advancement a sort of suicide. He started on the road to such rendering when he was very young. At fourteen, he attempted suicide by swallowing poisons, although it's difficult to tell how determined he was to die. At about thirteen, he had found his older brother's revolver and carried it from the Berkhamsted School (which he attended and of which his father was headmaster) to a local forest. There, he "put the muzzle of the revolver into my right ear and pulled the trigger. There was a minute click, and looking down at the chamber I could see that the charge had moved into the firing position. I was out by one." I suspect the cold-bloodedness of the writing is not only for effect: Greene's blue-eyed stare so often takes in death with equanimity. Its possibility seems to him and his characters a kind of relief.

He gave boredom as his reason for putting the gun to his head. The reason he stopped putting it there and pulling the trigger—after about seven tries, he claims, over days and weeks—was boredom with what had been the solution to being bored. He always sought ways of not being bored, and dangerous trips to savage and restless places became his favorite. He sought out danger and breeding places for fear because in contending with them he proved to himself that he was alive.

Like Hemingway, like Conrad, he fled the drawing room. Unlike them, he was very good at writing about the antimacassars and cooking smells and small rooms he and his heroes fled. So all of his work is a contest between the death in life that passes for safety and the life at death's edge that his protagonists need, paradoxically, if they're to survive. So make a moral, a psychological, map. Block in an oceanic need for faith and the need to evade it. For continents, sketch out the need for love and the helpless betrayal that love itself seems to cause. Add the need to help and the utterly human talent for doing harm. You have charted Greeneland. It is in West Africa; it is in Southeast Asia. It is always a place at the very edge, populated by characters themselves on the edge. Greene was drawn to boundaries. And then he had to cross them.

Here he is in revolutionary Mexico. His protagonist, a priest in the province of Tobasco, where the churches are closed and religion banned, has been traveling in disguise and has been thrown into jail. He despises himself. He is a drunk and the father of a bastard; he is convinced that he has utterly betrayed his faith. He thinks: "This place was very like the world: overcrowded with lust and crime and unhappy love, it stank to heaven; but he realized that after all it was possible to find peace there, when you knew for certain that the time was short." A woman in the common cell laughingly calls him a martyr, and he demurs: "I tell you I am in a state of moral sin. I have done things I couldn't talk to you about. . . . My children, you must never think the holy martyrs are like me. You have a name for me. . . . I am a whisky priest." Greene's achievement with the "whisky priest" of *The Power and the Glory*, the 1940 novel that remained a favorite of his (few could keep their author's affection), was to make a self-effacing and unholy man into something very like a holy martyr, and to make of his doubt and disgrace something heroic. He called into question verities on which civilizations had rested. He made of doubt a religious act worthy of admiration.

His evocations of doubters are successful in part because he evokes *place* so brilliantly. Here, from the 1947 story "The Lottery Ticket," is Mexico again. A middle-aged, middle-class traveler comes, searching escape from his boredom, journeying "in sickness and stench and the weariness induced by the wooden shelf they call a bunk." Greeneland is at once evident: "There were a few wooden huts, one little dusty plaza with a statue. . . . The buzzards rustled overhead, and out beyond the river the fins of sharks glided by. . . ." The traveler, a well-intended man who does harm as he seeks to do good, is in a place where "a sour smell poured up from the river, and a beetle struck his cheek and detonated off through the electric night. He heard it strike a wall." The man is made for us by the beetle detonating off his cheek and into a wall; that small, sensual specificity renders the man concrete; we can focus on him as if he were actual, and then go on to understand the climate of doubt he and his flesh engender.

Talking about Conrad Aiken, Greene used words that I would apply to Greene's own work: You can open his books "with all the excitement that comes from complete confidence in the author." So it is with, say, the Dickensian story of a small boy on his own and the two sad lovers who look out for him, *The Captain and the Enemy*, published when Greene was eighty-four, and so it is with the 1938 *Brighton Rock*, in which the brilliantly evoked killer Pinkie hears music that "moaned in his head in the hot . . . light . . . the nearest he knew to sorrow, as a faint sensual pleasure he felt. . . ." As that murderer is made actual to us, so is the policeman and lover and husband and Catholic in Sierra Leone—he is going to betray all of his beliefs—called Major Scobie, of *The Heart of the Matter* (1948):

> He lay on his back under the net and waited for her. It occurred to him as it hadn't occurred to him, for years, that she loved him: poor dear, she loved him: she was someone of human stature with her own sense of responsibility, not simply the object of his care and kindness. The sense of failure deepened round him. . . . There was silence all through the little house, but outside the half-starved pye-dogs yapped and whined.

In helping Scobie to dismiss himself for selfishness and imperception, Greene reveals him to us as decent and worthy. It is a masterful passage, a brilliant double whammy: We see the selfishness *and* feel the strength of the character, whose inability to understand his own worthiness we start to lament. The pye-dogs in their suffering become the voice of this complicated emotion.

Greene continued to write about boundaries all his life. He detested most of the international stands the United States took with regard to smaller nations—he saw our government as a bully—and he flayed us for Vietnam (*The Quiet American*, 1955), Cuba (*Our Man in Havana*, 1958), and Central America (*Getting to Know the General*, 1984). Considering the cross-Channel tunnel that breaches the boundaries of France and England, he speculated, in a story written in the 1980s, about terrorists mining the tunnel. They cause "deaths in the darkness, in the depths of the sea, death by mutilation and drowning."

In his border crossings, Greene can make comedy as well as mayhem. His 1982 *Monsignor Quixote*, a revisitation in contemporary Spain of the Cervantes story, with a confrontation of Catholicism with Marxism, holy vows with the pleasures of a bordello, offers a splendid scene in which Father Quixote blows up condoms like balloons. While we may laugh here, we must also be chastened by the powerful—the brilliant—honesty of Father Quixote, who, hearing a comedic confession from an undertaker who has stolen the brass handles from a priest's coffin, thinks this: "I didn't say the right words. Why do I never find the right words? The man needed help and I recited a formula. God forgive me."

The Father is a great man, as Greene was a great writer, because of that mistrust of self and the need to drive toward honesty. The prayer could be an author's as well as a priest's. And a later prayer in the novel could also be said by either, and by anyone drowning in the truth: "O God, make me human, let me feel temptation. Save me from my indifference." That "indifference" is the safety Greene spent his life fleeing. It is the danger he sought when he played Russian roulette, or voyaged into the most menacing places he could find.

Greene's fondness for telling stories about spies isn't surprising. From the start, he always saw himself, I think, as something of a spy—the unhappy schoolboy caught between loyalties in the school to which he felt condemned by his head-master father. He served MI5 and was friendly with Kim Philby, about whom he said, after Philby had fled to Russia and pub-lished his memoirs, "In Philby's eyes he was working for a shape of things to come from which his country [England] would ben-efit. Anyway moral judgments are singularly out of place in es-pionage." Again: the cold stare, the refuge of awful realism. John Banville, in his 1997 novel, *The Untouchable*, which fo-cuses on Anthony Blunt, portrays Greene as one of England's traitors, a spy for Russia all his adult life.

Greene tells of how, before he knew Philby had fled, he and a friend went to Philby's home. Greene's eye is as ever for the small, the evocative, and the slightly sordid: ". . . the floor under the door was littered with advertising brochures. In the kitchen there were some empty milk bottles, and a single dirty cup and saucer in the sink."

Doubt and betrayal are embodied, of course, in stories about spies and agents. His superb story "Under the Garden," which appeared in *A Sense of Reality* and which is found in the 1986 *Collected Short Stories*, offers this injunction to "Be dis-loyal":

> "It's your duty to the human race. The human race
> needs to survive and it's the loyal man who dies first
> from anxiety or a bullet or overwork. If you have to
> earn a living, boy, and the price they make you pay
> is loyalty, be a double agent—and never let either of
> the two sides know your real name. The same ap-plies to women and God."

The effort to hide in plain sight, to be a double agent *while simultaneously trying to be loyal*, sums up for me Greene's efforts as faithful husband, father, lover, worshiper, and storyteller. As Greene recalls from his youth,

Espionage is an odd profession: for some it is a vo-
cation, with an unscrupulous purity, untouched by
mercenary or even patriotic considerations—spying
for spying's sake. Already I had begun to be dissatis-
fied with the plain gathering of fact and rumour and
with its transmission to a single source; the idea of
being a double agent had occurred to me.

So, in *The Human Factor*, the trapped protagonist, a British
agent who serves the enemy for the sake of his beloved, is able
to save her life by spying on his English colleagues. He must
flee, however, and, having saved her, he can never be with her
again. He can only telephone from Moscow and possess his
Sarah with mere words: "She said, 'Maurice, Maurice, please go
on hoping,' but in the long unbroken silence which followed
she realised that the line to Moscow was dead." Greene, like the
Henry James about whom he wrote with insight and devotion,
was able to entangle his lovers, and then to express their love
through negatives: He forced them, with the mechanics of his
story, to prove their love by remaining separate.

Variations on this love in death, or proximity in separateness, run through so many of his novels, from *The End of the Affair* (1951) to *The Comedians* (1966) to *Dr. Fischer of Geneva*
(1980), in which a variation of Greene's Russian roulette is
played with explosive party favors, and a wonderful woman is
killed off early in the novel so that her widower will long for
death (and advance the novel's climactic moment).

Of course, as with loyalty, double agentry, religious yearning, and betrayal, Greene's themes over a sixty-two-year career
are repeated. So are the kinds of characters—weak men and
women who find unknown strength, large officials who are
hugely weak, the maimed and those blasted by fate. In *The Min-
istry of Fear*, an "entertainment" published in 1943, Arthur
Rowe, in London during the Blitz, hears in a German bomber's

engine beat "Where are you? Where are you?" In *Dr. Fischer of Geneva*, nearly four decades later, Alfred Jones recalls the bombing of London and the planes whose engines seemed to say "Where are you? Where are you?"

Over Greene's exemplary, monumental career, he carried on the work of the important traditional writers who told splendid stories, from Munro (Saki) to Kipling to the Buchan of *The Thirty-Nine Steps* to H. Rider Haggard to Chesterton and Maugham. Always part boy—hence his appreciation of Dickens—and always old man—hence his affection for James—Greene carried on and refined masterful storytelling.

He did not invent a new language or develop a sense of structure undiscovered before 1929. Instead, he set about to write with utter clarity, and with a simultaneous pity and contempt—for his characters and for himself—that made them recognizable, comprehensible, and interesting, and which yet always permitted them to hide (as their author wished to) the mystery at the core of their being.

His novels pull you in at once—"After dinner I sat and waited for Pyle in my room over the rue Catinat; he had said, 'I'll be with you at latest by ten,' and when midnight struck I couldn't stay quiet any longer and went down into the street."*
—and they insist upon remaining with you when they end—"I wrote at the start that this was a record of hate, and, walking there beside Henry towards the evening glass of beer, I found the one prayer that seemed to serve the winter mood: O God, You've done enough, You've robbed me of enough. I'm too tired and old to learn to love. Leave me alone forever."†

In his fiction's doubt and bitterness, there is also fine humor, and not only in *Monsignor Quixote* or *Travels with My Aunt* or *Our Man in Havana*. Stories like "May We Borrow Your Hus-

*From *The Quiet American*
†From *The End of the Affair*

band" echo with dark laughter, as does "The Lottery Ticket": "He headed for a door marked Dentista and flashed explanatory gold teeth. 'Pain,' he said with satisfaction, 'pain.' " That smile, those gold teeth, the hymn to pain—they are the awful jokes this universe, and its God, if there is one, play on Greene's characters' souls, who are determined to escape and who do not.

Neither does their author. In the autobiography *A Sort of Life*, Greene says, "For a writer . . . success is always temporary, success is only a delayed failure." He believed that, and he believed this: "There are faults in his work which he [the writer] alone detects . . . like a skilled intuitive builder he can sniff out the dry rot in the beams. How seldom has he the courage to dismantle the whole house and start again." Read "The New House," an early story, for a pointed elaboration in architectural terms of that artistic compulsion and that fear. Then read "The Destructors," a 1954 story, to see how Greene estimates the value of art to a maddened world: It is more bitter and frightening, in ways, than Golding's *Lord of the Flies*.

Greene was right that each book is a starting again. And he did have the courage and energy to start again so many times. And always, I think, he began with the fear that he might be motivated by, in his words, "the simple and terrible explanation of our plight, how the world was made by Satan and not by God, lulling us with the music of despair."

Whether that is precisely Greene's tune over that long lifetime in art, he remains for us, in the body of his work and the example of his bravery, one of the major writers for grown-up men and women, someone whose level gaze it might be interesting to try again to meet.

THE DESERT IN THE BED

I RETURN TO John O'Hara's "How Can I Tell You?" for the electricity of its dialogue, the pungent rightness of its details, the economy of its construction, and the sense of immensity O'Hara generates beneath its concrete matter-of-factness—what Auden describes in his 1937 "As I Walked Out One Evening":

> O plunge your hands in water,
>   Plunge them in up to the wrist;
> Stare, stare in the basin
>   And wonder what you've missed.
>
> The glacier knocks in the cupboard,
>   The desert sighs in the bed,
> And the crack in the tea-cup opens
>   A lane to the land of the dead.

/ 223

John O'Hara published about four hundred short stories in his lifetime, and since his death, during recurring periods of interest in his work, editors have found and published more. He was one of the most productive and, every once in awhile, one of the most brilliant and capable writers of short fiction in the history of the form. To readers of a certain age, he is identified with *The New Yorker*, where, until August 20, 1949, he published regularly. After that date—it marks the issue in which the magazine ran a negative review of O'Hara's novel *A Rage to Live*—he did not submit fiction to the magazine for eleven years. He claimed, in fact, to have stopped writing short stories in 1949 and, according to his Random House editor, did not begin to write them again until 1960, when he and the magazine were once more friendly.

"How Can I Tell You?"—a story that appeared in *The New Yorker* in December 1962, and that was collected in O'Hara's 1963 *The Hat on the Bed*—is a good example of what Lionel Trilling called O'Hara's "passionate commitment to verisimilitude," a manifestation of O'Hara's "brilliant awareness of the differences within the national sameness"—terms of praise one could well apply, by the way, to much of the work of Raymond Carver.

In a story called "Summer's Day," written during O'Hara's first great wave of short fiction, he creates Mr. and Mrs. Attrell, who encounter some local citizenry at the beach. Their daughter, it is revealed in a conversation overheard by Mr. Attrell, hanged herself. Wondering how he can ever again face the local man who spoke up for him and Mrs. Attrell, and wondering how he can in fact face his life, Mr. Attrell at last realizes "that there was really nothing to face, really nothing." The "nothing" with which Mr. Atrell is faced is both death and the death in life, the nada, of which Hemingway wrote in "A Clean, Well-Lighted Place." When he is at his best, O'Hara gives the "nothing" *and* the verisimilitude—Mr. Atrell drives to the beach in "a shiny black 1932 Buick with fairly good rubber and only about thirty thousand miles on it"—in a simultaneousness of effect that creates powerful resonance: The reader inhabits the fictive world's itness and emptiness at once. (It is when O'Hara is unable to establish the truth to his characters of "nothing" that his details overwhelm his work, and he produces banality—*A Rage to Live*, say, or *Ten North Frederick*, or stories smugly seasoned with trendy names and events and offering characters about whose fate we cannot care.)

"Nothing" is at the heart of "How Can I Tell You?" So are the details that make O'Hara at his best such fun to read. A student of American culture would have to consider our mercantile stories, from Melville's seed salesman in "The Tartarus of Maids," and his Confidence-Man, through those archetypal snake-oil salesmen of Twain's *Adventures of Huckleberry Finn*, the king and the duke, to Hemingway's "One Trip Across" and "The Tradesman's Return" (later incorporated in *To Have and Have Not*), to Faulkner's *The Hamlet*, to Welty's "Death of a Traveling Salesman," through Miller's *Death of a Salesman* and Mamet's *Glengarry Glen Ross*, to Raymond Carver's "Collectors"—and, surely, "How Can I Tell You?" would have to be part of this list.

It begins with the salesman's litany that knits it together from beginning to middle to end: "A T-Bird and two Galaxies," the selling of which mark a very good day's work. Mark McGranville is a veteran car salesman who in the course of a story laden with verisimilitude comes face-to-face with "nothing," or, more precisely, understands that he has been confronting it all along. (As in so many O'Hara stories and novels—and beginning with the Maugham parable about death that is epigraph to his first and best novel, the 1934 *Appointment in Samarra*—death or its cousin, "nothing," is associated with a woman.) A wealthy customer, Mrs. Preston, buys a red Thunderbird, with his initials painted on the door, for her son, a college boy. In the course of the transaction, McGranville and Mrs. Preston exchange crucial information in dialogue that suggests how much O'Hara admired Hemingway and how much students of the story ought to admire O'Hara.

Mrs. Preston, after inquiring about McGranville's mother, says casually, "Your mother's a fine woman, Mark. Any time she's thinking of going back to work again, I hope she lets me know first." So we know that the son of a house cleaner, climbing the narrow and slippery rungs toward middle-class "respectability," has been reminded—not only by Mrs. Preston's language but also through the contrast between his life and that of her son—about his origins. In telling Mrs. Preston about his mother's life with his sister, he says, "They have that little ranch-type out at Putnam Park, the two of them. Mary has her job at the Trust Company. . . ." And Mrs. Preston replies, "Very nice for both of them."

With her words in his head (and ours), he leaves work at the end of the day thinking that "all three sales should have made him feel better than he felt on the way home, and he did not know why he should find himself wanting a drink and, what's more, heading for Ernie's to get it." That's as deep into McGranville's thoughts as we will get. O'Hara shows him trying to get drunk and unable to, and he performs a little tour de force in writing Ernie the barman: ". . . for all-day drinking, I stick to scatch. You don't get tired of the taste of scatch. Your rye and your bourbon, they're too sweet if you're gonna drink all day. You know a funny thing about scatch. . . ." Just as much of the surface of the story resists our desire, and, indeed, McGranville's, for more information, so does McGranville's effort to learn what eats at him. He doesn't know, so he can't say. We end up saying it for him.

"He could not understand why he went through dinner and the entire evening without telling Jean about the T-Bird and the two Galaxies in one day." He does know that she would manifest pride if he told her, "and he was in no mood to share her enthusiasm or accept the compliment of her pride in him." That sense of adult sulking, and of the need *not* to be celebrated because of despair or unworthiness, is a wonderful perception by O'Hara, and it is touched upon with perfect glancing accuracy. McGranville cannot get beneath his mood to understand himself. His wife watches and listens. He kisses his children good night. He and Jean watch television until bedtime, when they go to their separate beds. There are only a few hundred words of the story left at this point, and it begins to unwind, like an anchor chain spinning out, with a low roar and with real danger to onlookers. Jean asks if there is something the matter. He says, "Nope." She says good night, and O'Hara—reflecting the formality between them—writes: " 'Goodnight,' said Mark McGranville." Ten minutes later, she says, "If you don't want to tell me." And he snarls, "How the hell can I tell you when I don't know myself?" So she knows, and he knows, and we know, and the problem is large and not apprehensible, though invisibly ballasted with Mark's history and the history of class separateness and its burdens. It—"nothing"—looms in the story.

Jean, who is perceptive and unbrilliant, offers to "come over" to his bed. Mark knows that he is too far from her to be reached: He says, "I just as soon you wouldn't." In a separate sentence, a perfect suggestion of the sad cadences of Mark's mind, O'Hara has Mark say, "I don't know what it is." Jean offers herself as a medicament, a sexual tranquilizer: "If I come over you'll sleep better." Mark then—perhaps because her generosity touches him, and surely because he is bewildered—explains to her, and to himself, the size of his unnameable predicament in the only terms they both understand: "Jean, please. It isn't that. Christ, I sold two Galaxies and a T-Bird today—" And their conversation—an enviable, sad, and beautiful bit of control by O'Hara that makes a writer's mouth water—dwindles away into talk of good sales days, the drink she smelled on his breath, his insistence that he wasn't hiding his drinking, hers that he did hide the news of his sales, and then her "All right. Goodnight" and his "Goodnight," the sad slide to silence that is part of one's sentence in life.

And they and we are left in the darkness of night and the inner darkness as Mark listens to his wife sleep and considers—because O'Hara can be a genius with details and because he knows that desperate people in the dark seize upon remarkable small matters in an effort not to drown in themselves—that she snores two musical notes, "the first two notes of 'Yes Sir That's My Baby'; the *yes* note as she exhaled, the *sir* as she drew breath." McGranville reflects—alerting us to his thought-provoked sleeplessness, their degree of love, and his perhaps surprising tenderness—how he had often watched her sleep, thinking that her sleeping face was not a mask but that, as he says, "The mask was her wakeful face, telling only her responses to things that happened and were said. . . . But in the frowning placidity of sleep her mind was naked. It did not matter that he could not read her thoughts; they were there, far more so than when she was awake." We might wonder why it "did not matter" that he couldn't read Jean's thoughts, until we understand that what matters to Mark is that "they were there": She was an authentic person, unreachable by him. If that is so, he is an authentic person, presumably unreachable by her (and by us). It is the fact of such separateness, the truth of solitude, that he seems to understand.

He gets out of bed, goes into the living room, and smokes a cigarette, thinking: "He was thirty years old, a good father, a good husband, and so well thought of"—do we hear echoes of Willy Loman's being "well-liked"?—"that Mrs. Preston would make sure that he got credit for a sale. His sister had a good job, and his mother was taken care of. On the sales blackboard at the garage his name was always first or second. . . ." "Nevertheless," O'Hara continues, "he went to the hall closet and got out his

20-gauge and broke it and inserted a shell." That "nevertheless" is of course what the story has pivoted on. It was introduced on the first page—the contrast between McGranville's dissatisfaction and the achievement implicit in "A T-Bird and two Galaxies." On the one hand, there is the arduous, long climb from the fringes of the middle class to something approaching its center; there are the emblems of success and even pleasure—the wife, the children, the house, the sister and mother "taken care of." On the other hand, there is what is always on the other hand, waiting to be rediscovered: the "nothing" that one wishes to evade, the emptiness that threatens to fill us.

McGranville returns to his chair. His cigarette has gone out, and he relights it—O'Hara is, here, the master of the small detail—and McGranville becomes a hard, heavy sculpture of confrontation with "nothing": "The shotgun rested with the butt on the floor, the barrel lying against his thigh, and he held the barrel loosely with the fingers of his left hand as he smoked." O'Hara uses the cigarette as a clock. We sense that when Mark is through with it, he will kill himself. Then: "The cigarette was now down to an inch in length, and he crushed it carefully."

As he does, "Her voice came softly. 'Mark,' she said," and her awareness, her *alertness* (corresponding to his less insightful alertness toward her, in her sleep), makes Jean the hero of this story. "He looked at the carpet." Here, O'Hara uses descriptive language to create a musical pause. His timing is superb. Mark finally answers, "What?"

Jean says, "Don't. Please?"

She calls him back to life, such as it is. "I won't," he says.

The dialogue has the weight of their history in it, and the heroism of Jean's comprehension and care. It says the avowals of love that their daily life cannot. It does not solve what Mrs. Preston has helped to reawaken in Mark, but it carries what comfort there is. The dialogue, like the events of the story, and like the story's protagonists, cannot say what the matter is, and they cannot say the solution. These people will never name their predicament; there isn't language for it.

Some of the importance of this story for me is its long look into what cannot be said and its confrontation of the silence in which and from which so many of us suffer. I applaud O'Hara's attention to the differences of class, the cost of money, the size of the distances that separate us. I admire O'Hara's accurate use of facts to create a plausible world. I am profoundly moved by the sad, strong, patient suffering of O'Hara's characters, and by the precision in its grappling with the silence of his characters' speech. I envy the abilities of this author, I respect his hard work, I am moved at times by his fear of insufficient recognition. I have tried to learn from his life and from his work about my own attempts to write stories about which readers will care.

This story of O'Hara's makes me hear the desert sigh. That sound is the reason I write.

HEMINGWAY'S SENTENCE

*I couldn't believe he was dead. When a reporter phoned me with
the news, I said, "Don't worry, he'll turn up again."*

—Morley Callaghan*

It is not fashionable to praise the work of Ernest Hemingway these days. His women too often serve his men, and they
so frequently seem to be projections of male needfulness. In a
time when "nurture" has become an ethic, a preoccupation, a
function, and a rallying cry—when it is the mother's milk of
people well past the milk-drinking age—Hemingway's characters are far less sensitive than we. On matters of racial and ethnic bigotry, there are too many examples of his lifelong

*In Denis Brian, *The True Gen* (New York: Grove Press, 1988), 263.

anti-Semitism, his affection for denigrating black people in just too many forums private and public. And he was violent: He loved the bullfights; he wrote of them with zeal, explaining away the cruelty to bulls and horses by celebrating how the matador danced with his death.

And he was just plain mean. As we reread *A Moveable Feast* and celebrate its fine prose and respond to its deep sorrows, we also experience Hemingway's ingratitude, his viciousness, to Ford Maddox Ford, to F. Scott Fitzgerald, to Gertrude Stein; and when we consider his treatment of Stein, we have to recall Hemingway's defamation of homosexuals.

He is so very incorrect, except in this: He gave the century a way of making literary art that deals with the remarkable violence of our time. He listened and watched and invented the language—using the power, the terror, of silences—with which we could name ourselves.

Often, he employed an apparently cocky but clearly shattered persona:

When they evacuated they had all their baggage animals they couldn't take off with them so they just broke their forelegs and dumped them into the shallow water. It was all a most pleasant business. My word yes a most pleasant business.

He admitted and did not admit, simultaneously, that what he spoke was nightmare. This persona contained the tension, as a nervous laugh contains a terrible cry, that was the heart of Hemingway's method. The voice he invented could generate the sorrow of the violence perceived while attempting to create repose, an instant's peace. The voice carried the violence and the flight from it simultaneously.

We can hear the simultaneity in the splendid opening paragraph of *A Farewell to Arms* (1929), a first paragraph that is a reworking of the opening lines of the 1926 story "In Another Country":

> In the late summer of that year we lived in a house in a village that looked across the river and the plain to the mountains. In the bed of the river there were pebbles and boulders, dry and white in the sun, and the water was clear and swiftly moving and blue in the channels. Troops went by the house and down the road and the dust they raised powdered the leaves of the trees. The trunks of the trees too were dusty and the leaves fell early that year and we saw the troops marching along the road and the dust rising and leaves, stirred by the breeze, falling and the soldiers marching and afterward the road bare and white except for the leaves.

What you think, as you begin it, to be a song of separateness, a pastoral, becomes a threnody. The celebration of the instant of love stolen away from time is dragged back into seasons and death—that dead bone-whiteness of the road glinting through. The paragraph is resonant, haunting, a poem: It contains the movement of the novel, it predicts the lovers' fate, and it then transcends their fate, on our behalf, by creating a moment that survives them.

Here is language with which to depict tragedy, I'd want a young writer to know. "Hills Like White Elephants," in which a very selfish young man tries to persuade a young woman to have an abortion convenient for him, can teach a beginning writer more about metaphor and about creating dialogue than a semester's attendance at one of several writing workshops I admire.

When he writes very well about love, loss, tenderness, or fear, Hemingway works with the assumption that he must cause the reader to share the unstated but very much sought emotion about which he is concerned. That is responsible writing, I maintain, a writing that is about the essential transaction between writer and reader. It is about being human in a time of despair—not simply about the vulgarities and weaknesses with which the large, swaggering man strutted through the world when it seemed, for a while, that he might own it.

Working at his best, Hemingway had no peer as editor of his own work. Read the chunk of lit-biz garrulousness he chopped away from "Big Two-Hearted River" before he published the story. (In its raw form, it can be found in Philip Young, ed., *The Nick Adams Stories*.) Consider the virtually Victorian ending he wrote for *A Farewell to Arms*—he offers a disquisition on each character as Frederic Henry drones away after Catherine's death—and which he then ruthlessly trimmed to:

> But after I had got them out and shut the door and turned off the light it wasn't any good. It was like saying good-by to a statue. After a while I went out and left the hospital and walked back to the hotel in the rain.

I honor that "After a while": He doesn't have to tell me outright that Frederic Henry weeps for his Catherine; the way he excludes the tears makes me taste them.

Hemingway is often codified, and then dismissed—yes, he requires that his protagonists behave with grace under pressure; yes, they must meet their moment of truth with composure. Right: finished, then, with *that* one. It is worth remembering, though, that he wrote about the making of art in the same way he wrote of fighting bulls or wars or big fish. That is, he made it clear to his readers that a writer who stared into the truths or evasions of the soul and tried to bring back something of what he had seen was a comrade-in-arms to the warrior or hunter in that each laborer at his trade offered his very life as stake in the plying of the trade. That is why I demand that young writers who work with me read Hemingway's work: It demonstrates that the making of art is a matter of life and death, no less.

At about twenty-four, I would say, Hemingway started to write about the choice his protagonists must make: either fall prey to the terror of living and therefore kill themselves or soldier on with what they might call professionalism. The choice was that severe. It was no metaphor. When he offered death as an alternative, Hemingway meant *death*.

He was the child of a doctor and a hardy, demanding artist (she had been a singer) who thought it important that their children see the dark facts of a difficult world. His father killed himself. Grace Hemingway sent her son a parcel that held a chocolate cake, a roll of her paintings, and the gun with which Clarence Hemingway had ended his life; she sent the gun because her son had asked her to. Hemingway's first wife, Hadley, was the child of a suicidal father. When Hemingway's leg was torn by a machine-gun bullet in 1918 and he lay bleeding from many wounds, awaiting an ambulance and in terrible pain, he thought, at eighteen, of shooting himself with his side arm. When he was leaving Hadley for Pauline Pfeiffer in 1926, he wrote to Pfeiffer of how he had thought "to remove the sin out of your life and avoid Hadley the necessity of divorce . . . by killing myself." A month before, he had written to someone else that "the real reason for not committing suicide is because you always know how swell life gets again after the hell is over." The dark call to die, and the insistence upon continuing, like the offering and withdrawing of emotion in his fiction, is the essential rhythm of Hemingway's life and art. He was a nexus for death. After he had killed himself, his sister Ursula committed suicide in 1966, as did his brother, Leicester, in 1982, and as did, in 1983, Adriana Ivancich, whom Hemingway had loved and on whom he modeled Renata in *Across the River and Into the Trees*. Recently, his grandaughter Margaux died of an overdose of drugs.

In his work, the expression of the dialectic begins in the story "Indian Camp" in *In Our Time* (1925). It is a small, simple story: a vacationing Dr. Adams, with his brother and his son, a very young Nick, is summoned to an Indian settlement in northern Michigan. A woman has been in agonizing labor for two days, and she suffers so loudly that "the men had moved off up the road to sit in the dark and smoke out of range of the noise she made." She lies on the lower bunk while her husband, cut so badly in the leg with an ax three days before that he cannot be moved, is pinned in place in the bunk above her.

Nick learns—he starts to learn—about birth and death. His father tries to explain about labor, and how the woman's contractions are related to her screams. "I see," Nick says, lying. And then the woman cries her agony again, and Nick begs, "Oh, Daddy, can't you give her something to make her stop screaming?"

This is a story in a book of stories in which women—and, surely, pregnant women—are invasive. It is a book that is in part about eluding women. But it is also the book of Nick Adams's education to more than men without women. So it is essential when Dr. Adams replies, first, that he hasn't any anesthetic, and then "But her screams are not important. I don't hear them because they are not important."

After the doctor performs a cesarean with a jacknife and catgut fishing leaders, and the infant is delivered, he examines the husband:

> The Indian lay with his face toward the wall. His throat had been cut from ear to ear. The blood had flowed down into a pool where his body sagged the bunk. His head rested on his left arm. The open razor lay, edge up, in the blankets.

Poised in his life above the edge of that razor is Nick, embarking on his education: ". . . sitting in the stern of the boat with his father rowing, he felt quite sure that he would never die."

When it was more usual to teach Hemingway, instructors liked to draw their students' attention to the razor in the blankets, its parallel to the infant swaddled in the bunk below: What's gained in life is also lost, they said; life and death, they pointed out, are born at once as realities to Nick—who hasn't yet learned to apply the lesson to his own life. (We might recall how keenly Hemingway wrote about learning and about teaching; even in *Islands in the Stream*, a lesser novel, the most affecting scenes are those in which Thomas Hudson teaches his child to fish; the African hunting scenes—moments of intense education—are the best parts published in *The Garden of Eden*.) Teachers might even have noted for their students that the last story in *In Our Time*, "Big Two-Hearted River," shows a Nick grown older, gutted by his experience of war, gutting male fish and leaving his knife—an echo of that razor's threat—"still standing," its blade stuck in a log.

What teaches me in the story, and what I wouldn't mind young writers and readers learning, is how, while Dr. Adams doesn't hear the screams "because they are not important," the husband *must* hear the screams: He cannot move away, like the other men, even if he chooses to—he is pinioned by his maimed leg; he is caught in his life. Of course, Dr. Adams does hear the screams, too, in fact; he's physically closer to the woman than her husband is. He is telling Nick, of course, that he *chooses* not to hear them. When he exhults over the success of his surgery, he also celebrates his ability to focus on his own psychic survival as well as his patient's.

These ruined legs, the therefore inescapable screams, are repeated in Hemingway's work. They provide the basis for his characters' choices—for Hemingway's measurement of the success of their actions and for their own measurement, too. Immobilized in pain and dread, they must respond to the screams that life forces from them or exposes them to by killing themselves; or they must find a way of diminishing the impact of the screams while still performing in their threatened lives with generosity, courage, and skill. They cannot flee "to sit in the dark and smoke out of range of the noise" except by taking their lives.

We are talking about a writer who made the ethos of his fictive world a matter of living or dying. He chose not to confine the trials and esthetics of his characters (or of himself as writer) to matters of comfort or ambition. He insisted that writing, which to him and his characters was risky and even heroic, was *itself* a matter of living or dying.

The equation of living or dying with writing well or badly continued—in *Death in the Afternoon* (1932) and *Green Hills of Africa* (1935). In his own voice and in those of his characters, Hemingway mingled discussion of how to write honestly with how to face death. It is during this period, in 1933, that Hemingway published the short-story collection *Winner Take Nothing*. It includes "Fathers and Sons," in part a response to his father's suicide, and a long story originally entitled "Give Us a Prescription, Doctor" but published as "The Gambler, the Nun, and the Radio."

He wrote it about a period during which, in a drunken afterdinner ramble, he repeated what he'd said years before: that "he would never hesitate to kill himself if conditions were bad enough." "Gambler" is rooted in Hemingway's experiences in a hospital in Billings, Montana, where he'd been treated for a broken arm. Because his protagonist, Frazer, a writer, who perceives the events of the story for us, must be held in place, the arm becomes a leg. He is in a good deal of pain but is "coming along good now since he spliced the bone"; he has been hospitalized for over five weeks—pinned in place by his wound, like the Indian husband—and he distracts himself with a little whiskey and a lot of late-night radio music. "When the nurse goes out I cry an hour, two hours. . . . My nerves are bad now," he admits to Cayetano, a gambler, shot in the leg and the stomach (the leg is paralyzed; he, too, is pinned in place). At the start of the story, Frazer hears a man, wounded in the thigh—we do not lack for legs here—scream all night long. Frazer's radio is a distraction from exterior screams, and from his own interior cries. "Usually [Frazer] avoided thinking all he could," but the cries get through. He and Cayetano, aspects of each other in their bravery and attempts at silence in suffering, agree on the code spoken by Cayetano: "Continue, slowly, and wait for luck to change." Meanwhile, Frazer fends off the screaming with his echo of Dr. Adams at the Indian camp: The pain, he says, "will not last, certainly. It is passing. It is of no importance."

No small part of Hemingway's artistic success and emotional appeal lies in his ability to announce pain and renounce it virtually in the same breath. He generates feeling and then his characters sheer off from it; he and his characters are alive to pathos and then labor to resist its attractions. It can be argued that his is the tactic of the child who seeks attention but who also wishes to avoid responsibility for having claimed it. It may be argued as well that the lover who labors to attract the beloved, and the artist who works for the affection or at least interest of the reader, may employ the same behavior.

The analysis is attractive, and it may be that during the heady moments of what has come to be called "demystification" in academic circles, some of that analysis may go on. Demystification is often employed (at least on the ground to which I have applied my ear) to scorn what the dead white guys have subjected us to for so long. Of course, it is also, at long last, only another method of calling someone a name, or removing from someone a label. The work remains, the art functions, and once we have praised ourselves for calling Hemingway a baby, we probably must come around to saying that the baby's fiction works awfully effectively on the soul of an attentive reader who is not rigidly, ideologically, insensible to it. We do feel the emotion in the stories, and we do feel the retreat from it.

It is 1936 now, and Hemingway, whose wife Pauline is very wealthy, and whose circle is, has come to regard himself with distrust. He feels that he writes insufficiently and that he has surrounded himself at his peril with the idle rich. He claims to be unaffected by accusations that he is insensitive to the needs of the masses, though he does bother to growl at his accusers. He writes a draft of a story about a writer named Henry Walden who is dying in Africa of gangrene contracted from a scratch on the leg. The story is called "A Budding Friendship," and it demonstrates ironically how the closer his death came, as "a friend," the closer the writer came to the authentic self he'd abandoned; for, as death approaches, the sick man, unable to held a pencil, "writes" in his mind: In spite of the screams, he tries, finally, to do his job.

Hemingway, in a later revision, abandons Thoreau, calls his writer Harry, retitles the story "The Snows of Kilimanjaro," and revisits his childhood, youth, and young manhood, concluding with an hallucinated voyage—it is ostensibly to rescue, but is really into death—that evokes Hemingway's own flight from the African plains to Nairobi when he was ill with dysentery.

At the story's start, when his wife asks how she can help him, Harry says she can take his leg off, "Or you can shoot me. You're a good shot now. I taught you to shoot, didn't I?" Since he is virtually paralyzed, her shooting him as his agent and student would be, effectively, his shooting himself. Calling his gangrene "the rot," and thereby evoking his moral deterioration as well, Harry says that rather than eat, "I want to write." That is his nourishment, and now that he is on the verge of death, it is the only reason he wants to live—to write what he has failed to write.

As he dies, he senses death: "It had moved up on him now,

but it had no shape any more. It simply occupied space." It has been, in his hallucinations, "two bicycle policemen . . . or . . . a bird"; "it can have a wide snout like a hyena." He is beyond images by now, however. Death becomes, simply, "it," and is only a weight on his chest, beyond his powers to name or describe. As he fails as a writer, he dies.

Hemingway had heard a story about a frozen carcass of a leopard on Kilimanjaro and had used it as epigraph to his story. It is *his* symbol, not his readers': We can assign a variety of meanings to it, but they do not add to the richness of the story; at best, they can please us by seeming to confirm what we feel Harry's failure and dreams to mean. The true meaning of the leopard, Carlos Baker quotes Hemingway as saying—its significance as "part of the metaphysics" of the story—is for Hemingway alone, I would suggest. He believed and said that the weight of a story is created by the bulk of it being known only to the writer. Hemingway's epigraph may well have been meant by him as Hemingway's epitaph. The image of the leopard dead on Kilimanjaro is part of his trying to evade the screams, perhaps, or part of his giving in to them. Surely, I think, the image is part of Hemingway's conversation with himself about his art, the matter of life and death.

And that is why at the end of *For Whom the Bell Tolls* (1940), Robert Jordan, a teacher, lies on the floor of the Spanish forest, "pulling hard on the leg, so the broken end of the bone would not come up and cut through the thigh." He is pinned in place by a leg so badly damaged that he cannot leave his post. He must delay the fascists, who are approaching, while his comrades escape and until their mission, the blowing up of a vital bridge, is accomplished. He loads his submachine gun, responds to the pain of his leg, and tells himself, "Oh, let them come . . . I don't want to do that business that my father did. I will do it all right but I'd much prefer not to have to. I'm against that. Don't think about that."

He is thinking, of course, about his and Hemingway's father's suicide and the need to ignore his own screams because, compared to his mission, they are not important. As the pain increases, he thinks, "Maybe I'll just do it now. I guess I'm not awfully good at pain." And then: "Listen, I may have to do that because if I pass out or anything like that I am no good at all and if they bring me to they will ask me a lot of questions and do things and all and that is no good. . . . So why wouldn't it be all right to just do it now and then the whole thing would be over with?"

Those doubts and fears, that pain, are the screams. Robert Jordan replies to them with "Because oh, listen, yes, listen, *let them come now.*" He prays for rescue in action that will kill him but that will not be self-murder. The dialectic goes on, the interior screaming, the refusal to obey the screams: "I think it would be all right to do it now? Don't you?" And then: *"No, it isn't.* Because there is something you can do yet." Jordan instructs himself to think not of his fear and pain but of his obligations, of his comrades escaping, of the woman he loves, of Montana. He meditates on the wound itself. And then the desire to die interrupts: "It would be all right to do it now. Really, I'm telling you that it would be all right." But he resists, telling himself, *"One thing well done can make—"* and then he stops. He has spoken as soldier and for Hemingway as writer. At that moment, the enemy comes into sight, and Jordan knows that he can perform his duty and be killed in the firefight. His final sensation, in the novel's last sentence, is "his heart beating against the pine needle floor of the forest." His death announces his life.

As I've been suggesting, I see a lot of criticism as name-calling and not very useful to the readers' understanding of how literature functions or to the writers' of how they could be better at their trade. I've no doubt we could talk of all these shattered limbs, and add of course the missing arm of Harry Morgan, the hero of *To Have and Have Not* (though his wife, Marie, alas for theorizing, attests to his virility—which we could, of course, call overmuch protestation by the author), then call ourselves Freudian, call Hemingway emasculated or fretful about his masculinity, and then not have to read him anymore. We could talk about social guilt, call ourselves Marxists and Robert Jordan an apology by Hemingway for being a class enemy, and then not have to read him anymore. We could indicate Hemingway's androgynous women, or women turned into "daughter," and discuss incest with strong mothers and sisters and clinging "daughters" and women whose haircuts make them seem like boys, and then not have to read him anymore.

This kind of dismissal, this filing away of writers in categories that trundle home like mortuary drawers, can, of course, extend to biography. We can call him a bigot and not read him. We can call him a depressive, the child of a depressive, a man who thought of suicide all his life, and then not have to read him anymore. Obviously, I'm in favor of reading him to learn from his art what he clearly was compelled to say again and again: that the refusal to hear the screams, to give in to them, was based on the need to perform the dangerous duty he saw himself as fulfilling—from the lifesaving delivery of "Indian Camp," when death is born to a boy, to the rear-guard faithfulness of *For Whom the Bell Tolls*. Each of these acts—the doctoring, the soldiering, the other activities, such as bullfighting and big-game hunting, that dominated Hemingway's life—was an analogue to writing, because writing mattered as much as living.

When the writing went badly, he must have thought more about killing himself. When he could recover his commitment and skill, the lure of dying must have receded. He was familiar with suicide all of his life, and he wrote best about it when he made an art that was a stay against it.

In February 1961, he was asked to contribute to a presentation volume for President Kennedy. Mary Welsh Hemingway remembers how he sat at the living room desk to write, and "in the adjoining kitchen I cleaned up our lunch things and fussed around with early preparations for dinner, thinking he would be finished any minute. At the desk Ernest was still bent intently over his writing."

After an hour, Mary asks if she can be of any help.

"No, no. I have to do this," Hemingway answers.

"It only needs to be a few sentences, you know," she says.

"I know. I know."

She recalls how "his pen hovered with nervous uncertainty," how a "sense of urgency, futility, almost a smell of desperation oozed out of him until, I felt, it clouded the big room." Driven out of the house by the tension, she goes for a very long walk. She then describes the scene she returns to: "In the sitting room Ernest was still hunched over the desk. A week later he finished the three or four simple sentences of tribute."

In the cobbled-together form of *The Garden of Eden*, which Scribner's ought to have been ashamed to publish in 1986, Hemingway writes this of his writer protagonist:

> When he finally gave up writing that day it was afternoon. He had started a sentence as soon as he had gone into his working room and had completed it but he could write nothing after it. He crossed it out and started another sentence and again came to the complete blankness. He was unable to write the sentence that should follow although he knew it. He wrote a first simple declarative sentence again and it was impossible for him to put down the next sentence on paper. At the end of two hours it was the same. He could not write more than a single sentence and the sentences themselves were increasingly

simple and completely dull. He kept at it for four hours before he knew that resolution was powerless against what had happened.

These brilliantly chilling words, icy and truthful, are about the death of narrative. Hemingway, a strong man grown frail, was finished and he knew it, saying so in the novel he had tried to write since 1946. It is wonderful to me that he tolled his death as a writer with such clarity and precision—that such good writing about writing does not seek analogy but instead is starkly about the panic and "complete blankness" that terrorizes writers.

I have talked about some of the plainest and most poignant examples I know of Ernest Hemingway's dedication to his art, which was hardly selfless and priestlike but which was, and this is my point, selfish and afraid. He did his work because it meant his life to him. His story as we may know it—from his letters, his conversations as reported by friends, lovers, and hangers-on, his fiction as we may choose to correlate it to his days and ways—is alive with death, and with his sense that he would inevitably reach out for it. What I have talked about is the obvious trail he left in his art of his lifelong movement between the most terrible sounds of life, and the final silence with which serious writers seem somehow to be familiar.

Hemingway, like each of us, was sentenced to his life. He had been able to endure it not by way of his roistering and the action into which he entered so furiously, but because of his art. He was doubtless all of the names that namers feel they must supply. He lived from that February day—during all of which he could not write several sentences—until the month of the anniversary of his birth, July. He killed himself with a double-barreled shotgun because a writer's life depends on doing the work. When that stops, the writer stops, too.

ABOUT THE AUTHOR

FREDERICK BUSCH is the author of twenty-one books, among them *The Mutual Friend, Harry and Catherine, Closing Arguments, The Children in the Woods,* and *Girls.* He is the Edgar Fairchild Professor of Literature at Colgate University. He and his wife, Judy, the parents of two grown sons, live in upstate New York.